Cambridge Topics in Geography Series
Editors: F. C. Evans and M. A. Morgan

The river basin

David Ingle Smith & Peter Stopp

# The river basin

An introduction to the study
of hydrology

CAMBRIDGE UNIVERSITY PRESS
Cambridge
London · New York · Melbourne

Published by the Syndics of the Cambridge University Press
The Pitt Building, Trumpington Street, Cambridge CB2 1RP
Bentley House, 200 Euston Road, London NW1 2DB
32 East 57th Street, New York, NY 10022, USA
296 Beaconsfield Parade, Middle Park, Melbourne 3206, Australia

First published 1978

Printed in Great Britain at the University Press, Cambridge


*Library of Congress Cataloguing in Publication Data*

Smith, David Ingle.
The river basin.

Includes index.
1. Watersheds. 2. Hydrology. I. Stopp, Peter,
1943–    joint author. II. Title.
GB980.S63    551.4′8    77-85688

ISBN 0 521 21900 0
ISBN 0 521 29307 3 pbk.

# CONTENTS

# ACKNOWLEDGEMENTS

Thanks are due to the following for permission to reproduce illustrations. The number in brackets is the figure number.

(16, 17, 18) R.C. Ward, *Principles of Hydrology*, 1967, McGraw-Hill Book Co. (21, 22, 23, 24, 25, 26, 36, 64) HMSO, *Surface Water Year Books*. (28) Northumbrian River Authority. (30) R.J. Chorley (ed.), *Water, Earth and Man*, 1969, Methuen & Co. Ltd. (33) D. Weyman, *Runoff Processes and Streamflow Modelling*, 1975, Oxford University Press. (38) B.T. Bunting, 'Slope development and soil formation on some British sandstones', *Geographical Journal*, 1964, vol. 130. (40) British Geomorphological Research Group. (50) R.J. Chorley and M.A. Morgan, 'Comparison of morphometric features, Unaka Mountains, Tennessee and N. Carolina, and Dartmoor, England', *Bull. Geol. Soc. Amer.*, 1962, vol. 73. (61, 62, 63, 71) Thames Conservancy, Thames Water Authority. (67, 68) Water Resources Board. (70) British Avon River Authority. (76) K.J. Gregory and D.E. Walling, *Drainage Basin Form and Process*, 1973, Edward Arnold Ltd. (77) Institute of British Geographers. (94) L.B. Leopold and M.G. Wolman, *River Channel Patterns: Braided, Meandering and Straight*, Paper 282−3, 1957, US Geol. Survey. (99) M. Morisawa, *Streams, Their Dynamics and Morphology*, 1968, McGraw-Hill Book Co. (100) Iceland Geodaetisk Inst.

The following were based upon Ordnance Survey maps with the permission of the controller of Her Majesty's Stationery Office, Crown Copyright Reserved: (29, 84, 85).

The photographs are reproduced by permission of Aerofilms Ltd (65, 83) and the Director in Aerial Photography, University of Cambridge (39, 66, 82, 92, 93, 98).

The jacket and paperback cover photograph of the mouth of the River Spey, Moray, Scotland is reproduced by permission of Aerofilms Ltd.

# FOREWORD

This book describes how to study the water cycle within a river basin. Taking as its central theme the factors which affect the flow of water in a river channel, it looks in turn at precipitation, evapotranspiration, soil moisture, the shape of the river basin, channel flow and floods. It then examines the movement of the river load and the different channel patterns produced. It introduces techniques which, while not exactly those used by professionals, will produce results of reasonable scientific accuracy within a very reasonable budget, and it contains a wealth of examples obtained from actual fieldwork.

It is written for sixth form and introductory college courses in geography or environmental studies and will be particularly useful for project work and for fieldwork in general, but it also contains examples and exercises for work indoors.

The authors would like to thank unsuspecting members of Field Studies Council courses with whom many of the techniques were first tried out, as well as their own former students who experienced the first throes of many of the attempts.

**1** The hydrological cycle: its elements of hydrogeomorphology

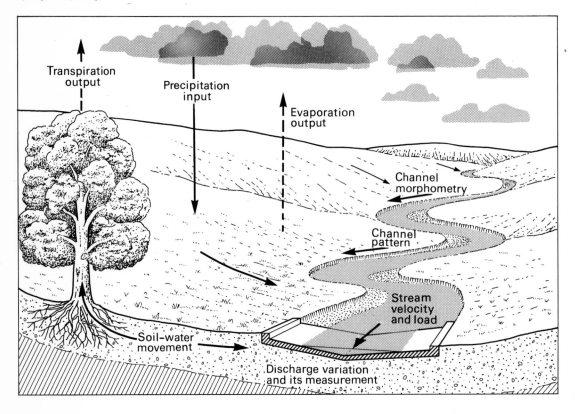

# 1

# The hydrological cycle

The elements of which the Earth and its atmosphere are composed
are contained within its atmospheric envelope. They do not escape,
neither are they added to. They are not static, but constantly move
from place to place and sometimes from one state to another. To
study our physical environment is to look at a changing picture. Our
landforms may appear virtually static relative to our own life span,
but they are in fact being operated upon continually by dynamic
processes. The study of these processes, rather than of the landforms
themselves, can lead us to greater understanding of how the landforms are produced.

The dynamic processes operating in our physical environment can
be seen as 'cycles'. Such cycles range in time-span and spatial scale
from the annual and localised growth and decay cycle of plants to
the very gradual movement of the plates comprising the Earth's
surface. Between these two in spatial scale, and very central to any
study of landscape processes, is the **hydrological cycle**, which is
concerned with the circulation of water at the Earth's surface. Its
fundamental components are precipitation, the movement of water
over the land surface and the return of water to the atmosphere.
These are shown in figure 1, where the terms used relate to the
contents of the various chapters of this book.

All the natural cycles interlock. Thus plants take up their
nutrients from the soil in solution with water, linking the nutrient
and the hydrological cycles. Similarly, the return of decomposing
humus affects soil structure and the ability of the soil to both hold
and drain water (chapter 4). Water draining through the soil layers
on a hillslope carries with it both weathered minerals in solution and
fine particles, thereby causing changes in the soil layers themselves
and also leading to erosion of the landforms. This links the hydrological cycle with rock formation, erosion and redeposition. Most
water finds its way into a stream course and it is there that the
eroded products are most easily collected and measured (chapter 8).
Such measurements provide one of the most useful means of finding
rates of erosion in humid lands, where water is the major erosive
agent. To make the calculations the catchment area of the stream
and its tributaries, and its drainage basin, must be studied (chapter
5).

Studying and, in particular, measuring the processes operating in
the landscape rather than simply describing landforms reveal the
degree of interdependence between elements in the landscape. The
interdependence of soil composition, its drainage characteristics and
the nature of its plant cover can be taken as an example. Removal of
an agent compacting the soil may have consequences for the local

plant cover as well as for the rate of drainage, which can itself have consequences elsewhere.

Understanding such interdependence enables us to predict the consequences of changes in the landscape, leading to more effective land use planning. For example, overgrazing a hillside slope can lead to soil deterioration and gullying on the hillside. It can also affect areas further downstream as increased erosion of headwater slopes provides more material for deposition. The more rapid run-off which results from compaction and gullying means a greater likelihood of flooding and possibly also of drought. In moderate climates without seasonal extremes of rainfall and, as a consequence, of river discharge, climatic hazards are rarely spectacular. However, in the increasingly crowded, developed countries of Western Europe and North America, the pressure on land is becoming more intense. Land values rise and more development takes place on marginal areas, even on those subject to occasional flooding. Consequently the effects of such hazards as droughts, frosts or floods become more and more costly and, as development schemes grow in magnitude and expense, it pays increasingly to be able to predict the likelihood of droughts and floods (chapter 7). Similarly, an understanding of the relationships between the factors which affect river flow (chapter 6), channel pattern (chapter 9) and river load (chapter 8) are important if any modifications to a channel are proposed.

Measurements of river discharge (chapter 2), precipitation and evapotranspiration (chapter 3) will add precision to hydrological predictions. For example, as explained in chapter 3, measurements of precipitation and evapotranspiration, combined with an understanding of plant moisture needs, make possible accurate prediction of irrigation requirements.

Figure 1 illustrates the aspects of the hydrological cycle that are examined in this book. It should be clear that we are restricting our attention to water on the land surface and are not considering the patterns of transfer of water vapour in the atmosphere or the movement of water in the oceans. Whilst we shall point out the relevance to Man of the study of aspects of the physical environment, we are concerned particularly with natural physical processes rather than human ones. Our area of study might therefore usefully be termed **hydrogeomorphology** — the study of the role of water in the formation of the landforms of the Earth's surface.

## Selected references

Hanwell, J.D. and Newson, M.D. 1973. *Techniques in Physical Geography.*
London: Macmillan.

# 2

# The measurement of discharge

In a study of a river the most important quantity is the river **discharge**. This is defined as the volume of water passing through a given cross-section of the river during a given period of time. The normal units for measuring river discharge are **cubic metres per second**, usually abbreviated to **cumecs**. For example, the mean annual flow of the River Thames at Teddington, Surrey, is about 77 cumecs. (For smaller discharges **litres per second (l/sec)** are sometimes used.) Formerly measurements were made in **cubic feet per second (cusecs)**. One cusec is equal to 0.028 cumecs. Water supplies are often measured in **million gallons per day (m.g.d.)**, one m.g.d. being equal to 0.053 cumecs.

There are a number of ways in which river discharge can be measured. The method chosen depends upon the size of the river, the accuracy required and the time and equipment available. The methods fall into three categories:

(1) dilution gauging methods;

(2) methods involving the measurement of river velocity and cross-sectional area;

(3) methods involving the construction of artificial stream channels or weirs.

A guide to the applicability of each method for rivers of differing discharges is given in table 1.

Table 1    *Applicability of techniques for the measurement of discharge*

| | Dilution gauging methods | Velocity/area methods | | Artificial structures (flumes or weirs) |
| --- | --- | --- | --- | --- |
| | | *Using a current meter* | *Using floats* | |
| *Large rivers* | Possible – but rarely used in densely-populated countries | Possible – but a cable-way is required | Can be used for recon-naissance work or in floods[†] | Not possible due to size and therefore cost of construction |
| *Medium rivers* | Possible – using dyes and sensitive equipment | Cable-way, bridge or wading methods* | Useful re-connaissance method[†] | Possible to use flumes with flows of 100 cumecs |
| *Small rivers* | A good method and possible to use with salt as the chemical involved[†] | Difficult if stream is shallower than about 30 cm* | Not very useful if stream is shallower than about 30 cm | V-notch and rectangular weirs are the most usual method[†] |

* Method suitable if some form of current meter is available
† Method needs relatively little equipment

3

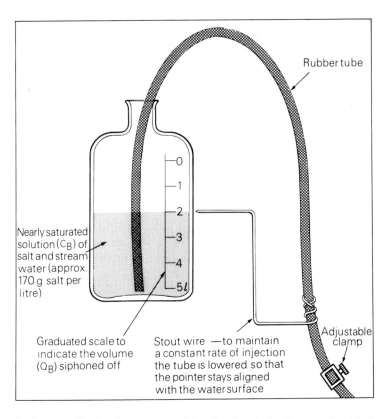

Figure labels:
- Rubber tube
- 0
- 1
- 2
- 3
- 4
- 5ℓ
- Nearly saturated solution ($C_B$) of salt and stream water (approx. 170 g salt per litre)
- Graduated scale to indicate the volume ($Q_B$) siphoned off
- Stout wire —to maintain a constant rate of injection the tube is lowered so that the pointer stays aligned with the water surface
- Adjustable clamp

## Dilution gauging methods

In these methods a known quantity of a chemical substance is added to the river and samples of the river water are collected downstream of the injection point to obtain information on the degree of dilution that has taken place. There are several methods using different chemicals and employing different injection techniques. For a review see Gregory and Walling (1973). Dilution gauging methods have been used in the United States on large rivers, for example the River Potomac, using fluorescent dyes such as Rhodamine WT (WT is an abbreviation for water tracing). The dye can be detected by its fluorescent properties in dilutions of 1 part in $10^{12}$ (i.e. 1 part in 1 000 000 000 000). Other methods use potassium dichromate or radioactive tracers. An inexpensive method for small scale field studies uses common salt (NaCl).

If a solution of brine of known concentration $C_B$ is fed into the stream at a known rate $Q_B$, and if, at a location downstream where complete mixing has taken place, the stream has a salt concentration of $C_{St}$ and a discharge of $Q_{St}$, then

$$Q_B \cdot C_B = Q_{St} \cdot C_{St}$$

Re-arranging this equation to isolate the unknown stream discharge, $Q_{St}$, we get:

$$Q_{St} = \frac{Q_B \cdot C_B}{C_{St}}$$

It is relatively easy to arrange the practical details of such an experiment. A nearly saturated solution of brine is made up using stream water and ordinary cooking salt. A rough guide is to use about 170 g of salt for every litre of water. The apparatus for the constant injection method is shown in figure 2. It is *essential* that the brine is fully mixed at the time

of injection; a small sub-sample is taken for the determination of $C_B$. To maintain a constant rate of injection the head of solution between the level in the container and the output end of the tube must be kept constant. This can be accomplished by attaching a length of stout wire to the tube so that as the solution is siphoned out of the container the tube is moved to keep the other end of the wire in line with the level of the solution in the con-

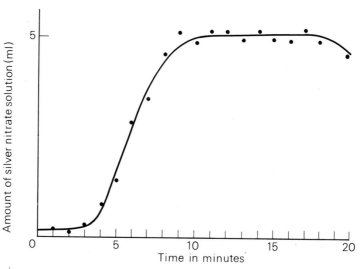

**3** Pattern of salt concentration in stream samples

tainer. The outside of the bottle should be marked in order that the volumes siphoned into the stream can be measured. Thus a value for $Q_B$ is obtained.

Samples of the stream water should be collected downstream of the injection point. The exact location of the collecting site will depend on local circumstances but the stream reach should be chosen to obtain complete mixing of the injected salt with the stream water. Ideally a straight reach of fast flowing water free from deep pools or backwaters is required. The method is very suitable for shallow, fast flowing upland streams, as complete mixing is essential for accurate results. On large rivers the mixing lengths are often several miles long; on small streams distances of 20–50 m are ideal if the flow is fully mixed.

Stream samples are collected every 1 or 2 minutes after injection, the sampling continuing for perhaps 20–30 minutes. After the field collection is complete it remains to analyse the samples for their salt content. This can be done by titrating the water for its chloride content, a procedure frequently undertaken in school and college chemical and biological departments.

The results are plotted as in figure 3. The objective is to define the pattern of salt concentration. In fact it is not necessary to actually determine the chloride level but to note the quantity of silver nitrate solution used in the titration. The sub-sample of brine is also analysed (it is usual to dilute this by a factor of at least twenty to help with titration; the result would need multiplying by 20 in such cases).

A sensitive electrical resistance meter connected to two open-ended wires which are immersed in the stream will show the plateau resistance of the stream water as the salt wave passes. A sample taken at that moment can be used. This saves considerable time as only one titration of the stream water need be made.

The ratio of the 'plateau value' from figure 3 to the value $C_B$ is then substituted in the equation together with the rate of injection, $Q_B$, to give the stream discharge.

The method of dilution gauging described, if undertaken with care, is potentially the most accurate technique for obtaining the discharge of small streams, but the discharge of the stream should not exceed 200 times the injection rate. There are other methods of obtaining discharge by the use of common salt which rely on the changes of conductivity rather than the determination of the chloride content.

---

# Velocity/cross-sectional area methods

The most usual method employed for the measurement of discharge involves determining the velocity of the river. If the river velocity (V) is multiplied by the cross-sectional area (A) of the active part of the river channel the discharge is obtained.
Thus:

$$Q = VA$$

where Q is the river discharge, V is the average velocity of the chosen cross-section, and A is the area of the cross-section.

A major difficulty encountered is that the velocity required is the

**4** Point velocity measurements and isovels
(cm/sec) for a stream cross-section

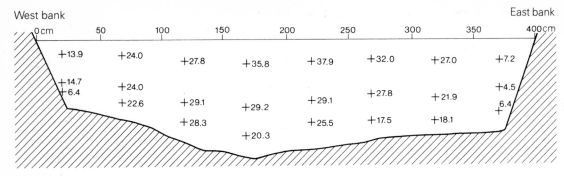

(a) Point velocity measurements in cm/sec

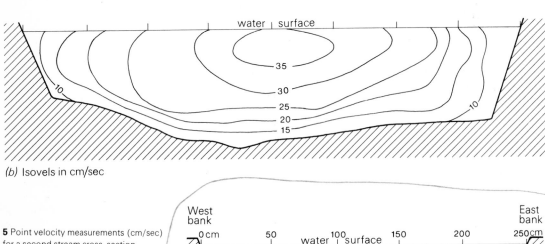

(b) Isovels in cm/sec

**5** Point velocity measurements (cm/sec)
for a second stream cross-section

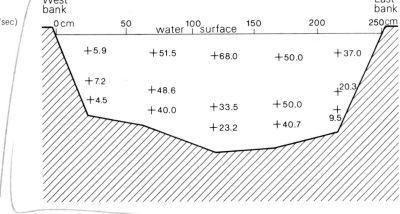

*average* velocity of the measured cross-section. The distribution of
velocity will vary considerably within any chosen cross-section. For
a straight reach of the stream the velocity is slowest near to the bed
and banks and fastest near to the surface in the centre of the stream
(see figure 5). If measurements are made of river velocity at individual points in a river cross-section it is possible to 'contour' the
diagram to show the locations of maximum and minimum velocities.
The contours, or lines of equal velocity, are known as isovels. Figure
4a shows a river cross-section with actual measurements of velocity
at varying points within the cross-section. Isovels based on these
point determinations are illustrated in figure 4b. Figure 5 shows
similar measurements for the same stream but for a different cross-

Table 2    *Details for the determination of discharge for the stream in figure 4*

| Distance from west bank (cm) | 0–50 | 50–100 | 100–150 | 150–200 | 200–250 | 250–300 | 300–350 | 350–400 |
|---|---|---|---|---|---|---|---|---|
| Row 1  $V_{0.2d}$ | 13.9 | 24.0 | 27.8 | 35.8 | 37.9 | 32.0 | 27.0 | 7.2 |
| Row 2  $V_{0.4d}$ | 14.7 | 24.0 | 29.1 | 29.2 | 29.1 | 27.8 | 21.9 | 4.5 |
| Row 3  $V_{0.8d}$ | 6.4 | 22.6 | 28.3 | 20.3 | 25.5 | 17.5 | 18.1 | 6.4 |
| Row 4  $\dfrac{V_{0.2d} + V_{0.8d}}{2}$ | 10.2 | 23.3 | 28.1 | 28.1 | 31.7 | 24.8 | 22.6 | 6.8 |
| Row 5  Area in square metres | 0.078 | 0.1224 | 0.1523 | 0.1699 | 0.1558 | 0.1413 | 0.1348 | 0.0983 |
| Row 6  Discharge in cumecs  Area $\times$ $V_{0.4d}$ | 0.012 | 0.029 | 0.044 | 0.050 | 0.045 | 0.039 | 0.030 | 0.004 |
| Row 7  Discharge in cumecs  Area $\times$ $\dfrac{V_{0.2d} + V_{0.8d}}{2}$ | 0.008 | 0.029 | 0.043 | 0.048 | 0.050 | 0.035 | 0.031 | 0.007 |

Notes: All velocities in cm/sec
Total discharge by $V_{0.4d}$ method is sum of values in row 6: 0.253 cumecs
Total discharge by $\dfrac{V_{0.2d} + V_{0.8d}}{2}$ method is sum of values in row 7: 0.248 cumecs

Table 3    *Details for the determination of discharge for the stream in figure 5*

| Distance from west bank (cm) | 0–50 | 50–100 | 100–150 | 150–200 | 200–250 |
|---|---|---|---|---|---|
| Row 1  $V_{0.2d}$ | 5.9 | 51.5 | 68.0 | 50.0 | 37.0 |
| Row 2  $V_{0.4d}$ | 7.2 | 48.6 | 33.5 | 50.0 | 20.3 |
| Row 3  $V_{0.8d}$ | 4.5 | 40.0 | 23.2 | 40.7 | 9.5 |
| Row 4  $\dfrac{V_{0.2d} + V_{0.8d}}{2}$ | 5.2 | 45.8 | 45.6 | 45.4 | 23.3 |
| Row 5  Area in square metres | 0.0963 | 0.1467 | 0.1731 | 0.1672 | 0.1102 |
| Row 6  Discharge in cumecs  Area $\times$ $V_{0.4d}$ | | | | | |
| Row 7  Discharge in cumecs  Area $\times$ $\dfrac{V_{0.2d} + V_{0.8d}}{2}$ | | | | | |

Note: All velocities in cm/sec

section. By placing a piece of tracing paper over figure 5 it is possible to draw isovels for this second cross-section. The relatively low velocity values near to the banks and the bed are due to drag between the water and the material forming the channel. This will be further discussed in chapter 6.

The problem is to obtain a pertinent average velocity for the river at a chosen cross-section. Hydrologists do not normally measure the point velocity values in as much detail as is shown in figures 4 and 5. They frequently use a simplification which can be considered as a 'code of practice' solution. They make the assumption that in any given vertical profile the average velocity corresponds closely to the velocity measured 0.4 of the way up from the river bed. This we can

7

call $V_{0.4d}$. For a slightly more accurate determination the velocity is measured at two points, 0.2 and 0.8 of the way up the profile from the main bed. The average velocity is then the mean of the two velocities. This is written as:

$$\bar{V} = \frac{V_{0.8d} + V_{0.2d}}{2}$$

where $\bar{V}$ is the average velocity in the chosen vertical profile.

The difference between these two determinations can be seen from a comparison of rows 2 and 4 in table 2, based on the point velocity measurements shown in figure 4a. A similar set of values can be calculated for the cross-section shown in figure 5 (see table 3). In general there is little difference between the two methods: the variations are greatest near to the stream banks where flow is slower and liable to eddy effects caused by the banks and the relative shallowness of the stream.

The actual measurement of the point velocities is undertaken using a **current meter**. Current meters normally consist of a propeller attached to a hydrofoil section. In a stream shallow enough to allow wading the current meter is attached to a wading rod. This is a metal rod with a base plate which rests on the stream bed. The rod is calibrated so that the current meter can be moved along it to the required depth in the stream channel. The number of revolutions of the propeller in a given time is then proportional to the stream velocity. The revolutions are counted by a small electric counter and, by means of a conversion table, are converted to give the stream velocity.

In larger rivers a cable-way is used from which the current meter is lowered to a predetermined depth.

Every effort should be made to select a straight reach of the stream with a well defined channel, free of weeds and other obstructions. Once the cross-section has been chosen it is necessary to measure its shape. For a small stream the best procedure is to extend a measuring tape across the river and make a series of vertical measurements at regular intervals.

The velocity is then determined with the current meter set at the appropriate depths for a number of equally spaced profiles. The number of vertical profiles selected depends both on the nature of the cross-

section and the time available. Eight profiles were used in figure 4 and five in figure 5. The discharge between any two vertical profiles should ideally not exceed 10% of the total discharge over the whole cross-section. For detailed work twenty or more profiles may be required. A decision about how many profiles to make clearly needs to be made before starting the measurements, and it may be useful first to make some quick approximations from a few measurements spaced out across the channel so that the required number of profiles can be judged more accurately.

*Calculation of discharge*

It is a relatively simple matter to calculate the discharge using the velocity and cross-sectional area measurements. The simplest method is to draw the cross-section to scale on a large sheet of graph paper, and to mark in the equally spaced profiles at which the velocity was determined. Then the discharge of the stream is considered for each part of the cross-section. For the discharge of ABFE on figure 6 the cross-sectional area ABFE is multiplied by the mean velocity in the profile XY. The area is obtained by counting the squares forming the area ABFE on the graph paper. This is repeated for the whole area of the cross-section and the sum of the discharges for each part of the full cross-section gives the total discharge of the stream.

Table 2 gives the data for velocity and area and the calculation of discharge for the stream cross-section of figure 4a. Table 3 is partially completed for a differing cross-section of the same stream using the

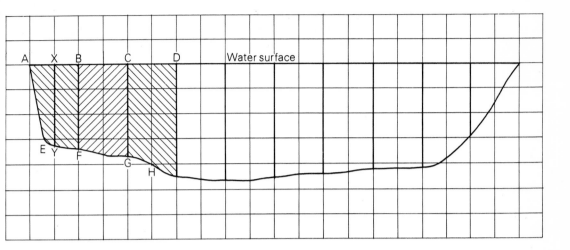

data given in figure 5. It can be used to calculate the total discharge
for this cross-section. Compare the results with those in table 2.
Theoretically and in practice they should be very similar! It is worth
commenting that even with a good quality current meter errors of 5
to 10% are not unusual. Tables 2 and 3 compute the total discharge
using both the $V_{0.4d}$ and $(V_{0.2d} + V_{0.8d})/2$ methods. The resultant
discharge values vary slightly but the calculations using the velocity
at 0.2 and 0.8 of the depth should be more accurate. The reason for
this is apparent when the isovel pattern for the channel cross-section
in figure 4b is considered.

*Float measurements*
Current meters are expensive instruments and an alternative method
for the measurement of velocity involves the use of **floats.**
    The simplest form of float measures the surface velocity of the
river. Detailed studies of the distribution of velocity in a channel
cross-section show that the surface velocity in a given vertical profile
is greater than the average velocity for that profile (see figures 4a
and 5). A generally accepted conversion factor is that the mean
velocity in any given vertical profile is 0.85 times the surface velocity.
So if the surface velocity can be measured by the use of floats it is
possible to calculate the total discharge of the stream by the velocity/
cross-sectional area methods outlined already.

It should be stressed that float
methods of this type are less accurate
than the use of current meters and a
variety of practical field problems are
encountered. It is essential that the
float should be constructed so that
it travels completely submerged. This
is important because wind and ripple
effects can cause considerable errors
if a portion of the float protrudes
above the water surface. The length
of the float should be short, 10–
15 cm, unless the stream is very

shallow. Simple, inexpensive rod
floats can be constructed from
wooden dowelling with a diameter of
5–10 mm, and weighted so as to
float just below the water surface.
The rod can be weighted by wrapping
garden wire around the lower end.
Small plastic phials or bottles weighted
with lead shot are a simple alternative.
    The method is to select a reach of
the stream from 10 to 50 m in length.
The reach must be as straight as
possible, and ideally should have a

constant cross-section. The float is
dropped into the selected portion of
the stream and timed over the
measured length. Repeated runs
should be made over each selected
stream reach and a mean surface
velocity value obtained. This mean
velocity is then multiplied by 0.85
to give the average stream velocity
for that profile.
    This procedure should be repeated
for several vertical profiles across the
stream in a similar manner to those

9

using current meter methods. Subsequent calculations are as for the previous section where velocity was measured using a current meter, the only difference being that the cross-sectional area used should be the mean over the length of the reach used. The problems are that streams are rarely straight or maintain a constant width and floats used near the banks frequently become caught up in small side eddies.

The use of floats as described above gives, at best, only an approximation of actual stream discharge. However the method is occasionally used by professional hydrologists. Such methods are used during floods when it is necessary to obtain an estimate of discharge by quick and simple means. Discharge values for floods are of major importance and frequently the use of the standard gauging techniques is impossible at such times.

## Artificial structures

Artificial structures used for the determination of river discharge are **flumes** (figure 7) and **weirs**. The principle of measurement is the same in both cases in that the flow of the river is channelled through a cross-section of known dimensions and the depth of water flowing over the cross-section corresponds to an already known discharge. A graph is used to convert the depth of water (**stage**) to discharge. Conversion graphs of this kind are known as **stage/discharge rating curves**. Since the artificial structures are constructed to detailed specifications the rating curve is standard for weirs or flumes of a particular type, though in practice the rating is frequently checked using the velocity/cross-sectional area methods discussed already. Large stream flumes of the type illustrated are extremely expensive to construct.

Such flumes are sometimes used on rivers to measure flows as great as 100 cumecs but the same principle can be applied to the

measurement of discharge of very small streams. In this case a **thin plate weir** (figure 8) is used, rather than a stream flume which is a section of artificial stream channel. A weir plate acts as a dam placed across the stream and the flow passes through a shape of known cross-section. Stage/discharge rating curves have been published for a variety of types of cross-sections for thin plate weirs, including rectangular and V-notch types. It is possible with a minimum of practical skill to make and install weirs of this kind on small streams.

The most useful simple weir plate for the measurement of small stream discharge is a V-notch weir with the angle of the V being 90°. The head of water flowing over the weir plate corresponds to the discharge of the stream. The relationship between the head of water and the discharge for a V-notch weir is given by the equation:

$$Q = 1336H^{2.48}$$

where Q is the discharge in litres per second and H is the head of water in metres.

If the weir is constructed with H equal to 50 cm the maximum discharge that can be measured before the weir is overtopped is 240 l/sec and the minimum flow that can be measured is about ½ l/sec.

Substitution of the height (H) into this equation for each observation is a tedious procedure and normally a conversion graph (rating curve) of

11

**9** Conversion graph to find discharge from readings of the head of water over a 90° V-notch weir

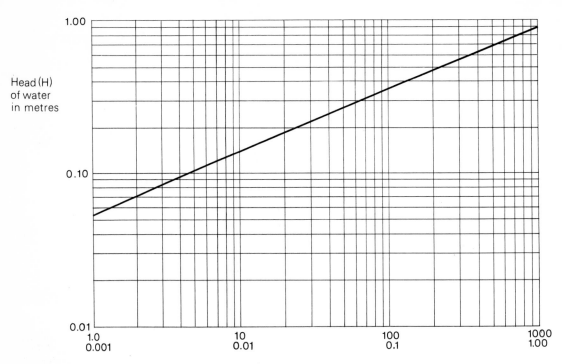

Head (H) of water in metres

Discharge (Q) in litres per second or cubic metres per second

head plotted against discharge is used. A rating curve for a 90° V-notch weir is given in figure 9. It is plotted on logarithmic graph paper, for an explanation of which see the appendix.

A useful account describing the installation of a small permanent weir for geographical field studies is given by Gregory and Walling (1971). Reliable measurements can be obtained by constructing a weir out of sheet metal or thick perspex. When the water flows over a weir of this kind there is a draw-down effect over the weir plate and if accurate measurements are required the head of water should not be measured in the notch itself. Figure 10 illustrates the draw-down effect and shows a **stage pole** from which the head (H) of water flowing over the weir is read.

Equations are available for other weir shapes, and these are reviewed by Gregory and Walling (1973). The formula for a rectangular weir is:

$$Q = 1837 (L - 0.2H) H^{1.5}$$

where Q is the discharge in litres per second, L is the width of the rectangular weir in metres, and H is the head of water flowing over the weir in metres.

If a rectangular weir is constructed with a width of 150 cm and a height of 50 cm, the maximum discharge that can be measured is some 600 l/sec and the minimum flow about 25 l/sec.

The V-notch is of more general application for the measurement of small stream discharge, as for low flows the head increases more rapidly than for high flows. It is best restricted to small streams where the head of water is unlikely to exceed about 50 cm.

*River stage*

Where regular observations are required on the discharge of a stream, or river, a rating curve is constructed to give the relationship between river level (stage) and the discharge. In this case a stage pole (figure 8) is installed at the beginning of the period of observations. The divisions marked on the stage pole are not important but are normally in metric units. The stage pole should be firmly installed so that it will not be washed away in floods. An essential precaution is

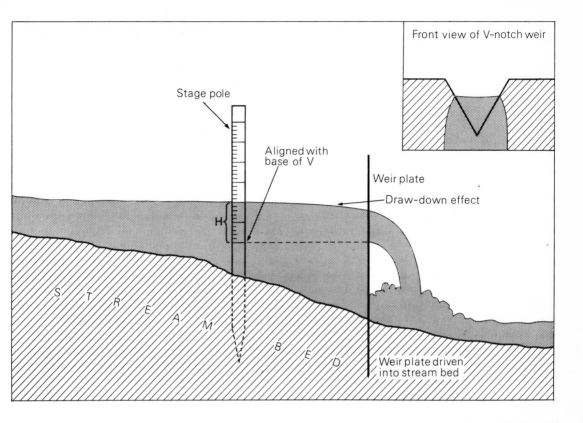

Front view of V-notch weir

Stage pole

Aligned with
base of V

Weir plate

Draw-down effect

H

STREAM
BED

Weir plate driven
into stream bed

to make sure that if the stage pole is destroyed a replacement can be
established in exactly the same position as the first. If flow measurements are being made near to a bridge the brick courses can be used
as a rough and ready measure of stage.

The stage pole is used to measure the river level. The river discharge is measured on given occasions and the stage levels also carefully noted and a rating curve built up.

One advantage of the stage/discharge relationship is that immediately the stage pole has been established readings can commence and
can be converted to discharge values at a later date when a stage/
discharge rating curve has been produced. When gauging stations are
installed to measure river discharge they are often fitted with a
continuously recording stage recorder (figure 7). A large float is
housed in a **stilling well** to reduce the effects of wind ripples and
surface disturbance. As the float moves up and down in response to
changes in stage, it rotates a drum along which a clock-driven pen
records readings over a week. These readings can be converted to
discharge by use of the rating curve for the site. Modern recorders
use punch tape recording methods, and the tape is fed directly to the
computer to obtain discharge.

A detailed network of continuous stage recorders is established in
the British Isles as in other countries. The recorders are maintained
by the Regional Water Authorities (formerly by the River Authorities) and all the records are assembled by the Water Resource
Centre at Reading. These records form the basis for all national planning that involves water resources. Summaries from the records of all

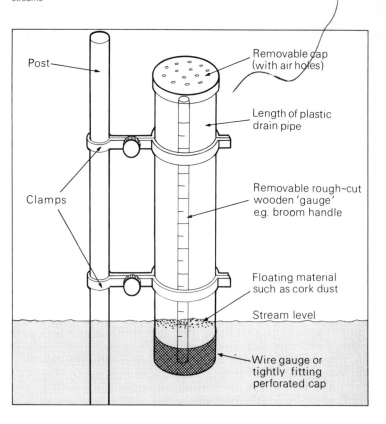

**11** Maximum stage recorder (or crest stage gauge) suitable for use on small streams

Post

Removable cap (with air holes)

Length of plastic drain pipe

Clamps

Removable rough–cut wooden 'gauge' e.g. broom handle

Floating material such as cork dust

Stream level

Wire gauge or tightly fitting perforated cap

The plastic drain pipe in the figure is clamped to a post or to the bank at a suitable height for recording high flows. The lower end is placed in the stream and covered with perforated material to allow water to enter. As water rises in the pipe the floating cork dust, plastic chippings, coffee grounds, or similar substance, rise and 'record' the maximum stage by a 'tide mark'. The wooden stick is removed to read the stage and this is converted to discharge using a rating curve for the site. To reset the marker it is wiped clean and the stilling well is topped up with more floating material. Use of the results is described in chapter 7.

major rivers are published in the *Surface Water Year Book of Great Britain* (see table 7).

The construction of a continuous stage recorder is an ambitious undertaking, but it is possible to construct a **maximum stage recorder** (or **crest stage gauge**). This enables the maximum stage attained in a given flood to be recorded. Maximum flows are of particular significance in many hydrological investigations (see chapter 7) and the instrument is shown in figure 11.

Measurements of discharge are an essential ingredient for any hydrological study and as with many field observations it is difficult to obtain precise values. Once discharge measurements have been obtained interest centres on explaining the values obtained and on using the results in solving practical problems. Chapters 3 to 6 examine the journey of water towards the gauging station in order to see what influences river discharge, and chapters 7 to 9 look at relationships between discharge and river load, discharge variations and channel patterns related to discharge.

### Selected references

BSI. 1964. Methods of liquid flow in open channels. *British Standard 3680*, part 3. London: HMSO.

Gregory, K.J. and Walling, D.E. 1971. Field measurements in the drainage basin. *Geography*, **56**, 227–92.

Gregory, K.J. and Walling, D.E. 1973. *Drainage Basin Form and Process: A Geomorphological Approach*. London: Arnold.

# 3

# Inputs and outputs of the river basin

It is clear that changes in the discharge of rivers are related to variations in precipitation. The relationship, however, is complex. For example, few rivers or streams cease to flow after even prolonged periods of drought so there must be a 'store' of water which enables the stream to continue to flow. Also there is a time lag between the onset of heavy rain and an increase in discharge. In this and succeeding chapters the term 'run-off' will be used frequently and requires some explanation here.

**Run-off** is the name given to the total discharge of a river over a given time period — usually a day, a month or a year — converted to the equivalent depth of water spread over a plane equal to the area of the river basin. Thus, for a basin such as the River Blithe above Hamstall Ridware, Staffordshire, with its area of 162 km$^2$ and a mean discharge of 2.92 cumecs for the month of January, the run-off for January is found by multiplying the mean discharge per second by the number of seconds in that month and dividing by the basin area in m$^2$:

$$\frac{2.92 \times 60 \times 60 \times 24 \times 31}{162 \times 1000 \times 1000} = 0.0483 \text{ m}$$

The result is directly comparable with rainfall, and to facilitate this comparison run-off is usually expressed in millimetres — 48.3 mm in this example.

The rainfall/run-off relationship of the hydrological cycle can be considered as a system of stores and links. This system (shown in figure 12) consists of an **input** of the various forms of precipitation, of which rain is the most important, and an **output**. The final output is largely composed of river run-off, although in some cases the output can leave the river basin as groundwater. An input—output system of this kind is sometimes referred to as a **black box model**. The term 'black box' indicates that although the inputs and outputs are known the details of what goes on between input and output are not known.

This chapter describes the input to the system, precipitation, and also considers interception. So the inputs and outputs of the black box will be those taking place at ground level. The outputs will also be considered so that we can find the total loss that occurs within the river basin. Such losses will be mainly due to evapotranspiration.

## Input: precipitation

**Precipitation** represents the part of the hydrological cycle about which most information is available. There are over six thousand rain gauges in Great Britain that are read daily and the data from these are published by the Meteorological Office in *British Rainfall*. The

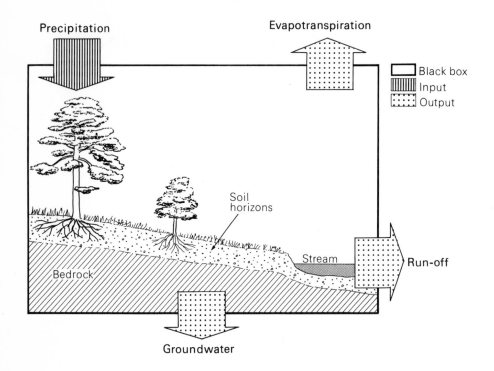

method of measurement is simple and the standard rain gauge consists of a copper funnel, diameter 12.5 cm (5 in), fitting over a copper cylinder in which there is a bottle to catch the water. The gauge is normally read each day at 09.00 hrs, the contents of the bottle being poured into a specially graduated measuring cylinder. The precipitation is recorded as millimetres of 'rainfall' over a 24-hour period.

The gauge is sited in open ground, away from obstructions, with its collecting funnel 30 cm (12 in) above the ground surface. Recent detailed studies have indicated that a gauge of this type tends to give a slight underestimate of rainfall. This underestimate is due to the turbulence of the air flowing around the gauge. Recording gauges of various patterns are also available and these operate like a barograph, producing a trace on a chart which gives details of both the time and the intensity of the rainfall.

A complication occurs when precipitation is not in the form of rain. It is difficult to measure the amount of snowfall and convert it satisfactorily to its water equivalent. The usual method in Britain, which is unsatisfactory, is to allow snowfall to collect in the funnel of the rain gauge and then if it has not already melted, to melt it at the time of observation. Turbulence is a very severe problem in measuring snowfall, not to mention the problem when the gauge is completely buried. The alternative is to abandon the gauge method completely when heavy snow occurs and to measure the average depth of snow that has fallen in the previous twenty-four hours, recording this as a water equivalent. A very approximate conversion

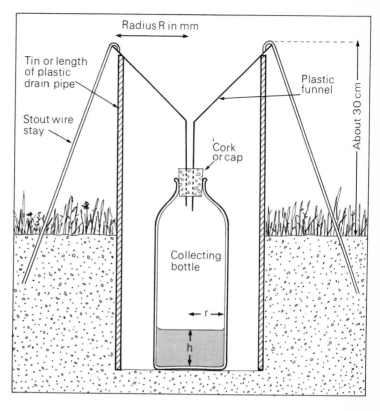

is that 10 cm of snow is the equivalent of 1 cm of rainfall. The contribution of dew or hoar frost to precipitation is even more difficult to evaluate. In Britain the effect of dew is likely to be small, but it is of great importance to farming in arid areas such as southern Israel.

*Rain gauge measurements*
Despite these shortcomings, the standard rain gauge does represent a very simple method for the collection of rainfall data. A gauge can be easily and cheaply made by using a plastic funnel and a bottle. It is best if the bottle is placed in a container, for example an old tin, with the funnel resting on the rim and further secured on the bottle by a cork or cap, for example of plasticine (see figure 13). This arrangement makes the funnel stable in windy conditions and the cap to the bottle cuts down possible evaporation losses.

A possible exercise is for each member of a class to construct his own rain gauge (the only real cost is likely to be for a cheap plastic funnel) and to set it up at home. Observations can be made once a day and the results plotted on a map of the local region. If the plastic funnels are all of the same size for the class, all that is required is a measurement, in millimetres, of the volume of rainfall. The results can be graphed to make conversion quicker. If the same bottle containers are used throughout as well as standardised funnels, the conversion is even easier and consists only of measuring the depth of water in the bottle. It is quite simple, however to convert the readings to depths of rainfall if desired. If a straight-sided collecting bottle is used the true rainfall (H) is given by the formula $H = r^2 \cdot h/R^2$, where the letters refer to those used in figure 13.

If such measurements are carefully made over a period of a few weeks, daily or weekly totals can be plotted on a large scale map of the district from which local rainfall variations can be seen. Figure 14

**14** Rain gauge observations showing local variations in precipitation on various days, Jamaica

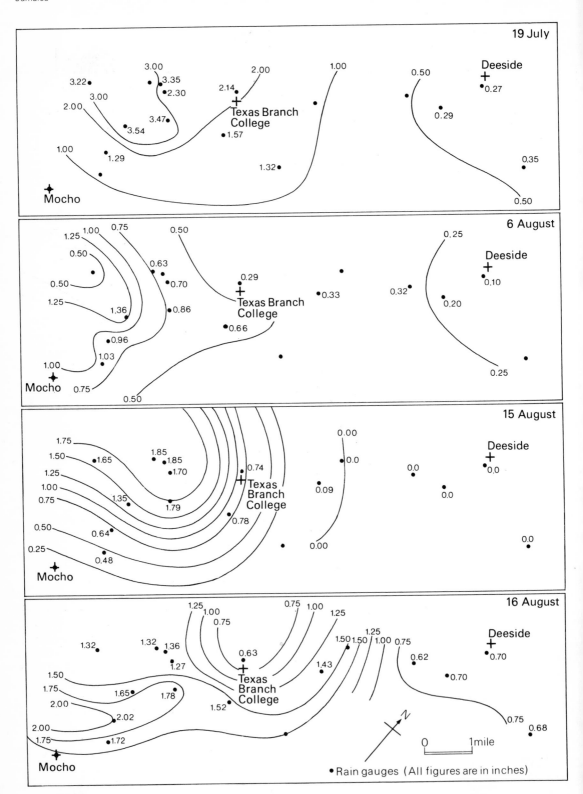

shows plots from simple rain gauges of the daily rainfall for an area in Jamaica. The rain on each day was from one storm and the track of the storm across the area can be seen. Tropical storms may show more local variations than occur in more temperate climates, but there are variations in these climates, especially if the area under study is large and of varied relief.

Investigations may also be made into the effects of obstructions on rainfall catch. A series of gauges can be situated at varying distances from a major obstruction, e.g. a high wall, to study the effects that it has on rainfall. The literature suggests that the effects should not be noticeable at distances of ten times the height of the obstruction. This varies, however, with the density of the

obstruction, e.g. it differs for a wall and a hedge of the same height.

Such an experiment is of greater value if information on the direction and strength of the wind associated with the rainfall is available. The network of gauges could, for a suitable site, be extended to both sides of the obstruction.

## Interception

Rain under most conditions does not fall directly upon the ground but is affected by the branches and foliage of plants. This is termed **interception**. Precipitation caught on vegetation can follow three possible routes. First, it can drip off the plant leaves to reach the ground beneath and so join surface and soil water movement. This is known as **throughfall**. In the case of rain intercepted by trees further interception can occur at a lower level which is termed **secondary interception**. Secondly, the rain may run along leaves and branches and finally reach the ground by running down the major stems of the plants. This effect is the same whether the vegetation consists of trees or smaller plants such as grasses, and the process is termed **stemflow**. Thirdly, the rain intercepted by vegetation may be lost by **evaporation** from the plant leaves and returned directly to the atmosphere. The processes are illustrated in figure 15. In this

**15** Flow diagram showing interception, stemflow and throughfall

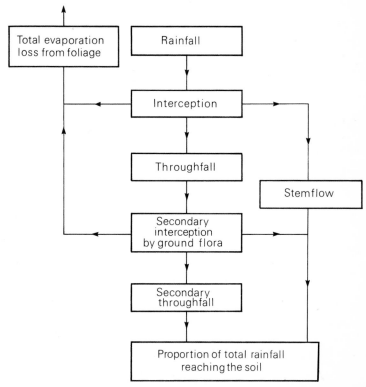

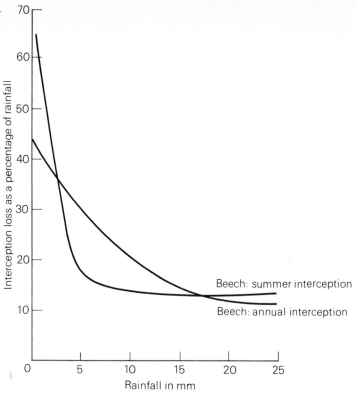

**16** The percentage interception loss for beech trees

Interception loss as a percentage of rainfall

Beech: summer interception

Beech: annual interception

Rainfall in mm

chapter we will only be concerned with the direct loss due to these interception processes. Surface and soil water circulation will be considered in chapter 4.

Interception is difficult to measure although its effect is easy to demonstrate. A rain gauge can be set up beneath differing vegetation types and the results compared to the rain catch in a similar gauge situated in an open site. It needs little imagination to realise that one rain gauge beneath a large tree will give only a very general idea of the overall interception loss. In other words the spatial variations in throughfall are considerable. Interception will vary not only with the siting of individual rain gauges but also with the type of vegetation, the season of the year, the intensity of the rainfall, wind speeds and temperature.

The values for interception given in the literature show very considerable variation but figure 16 illustrates the general principles. The interception from beech trees in the summer for light rain can be very large, but for storms with higher rainfalls the interception loss tends to level out at about 15%. The annual figures (an average of summer and winter conditions) for beech are very much less for light rain and this is due to the loss of foliage in the winter. Most workers agree that coniferous trees have a higher interception loss than deciduous trees even during the summer. It would appear that drops of water find it easier to cling to individual needles but tend to flow more easily from large deciduous leaves.

Tropical evergreen rain forest, with its close crown cover of vegetation, is thought to have an interception loss of 30%, whilst 46% of the precipitation reaches the ground by stemflow and 24% as throughfall.

A broad average for the interception loss under a grass cover would be about 20% of the total precipitation. Agricultural crops

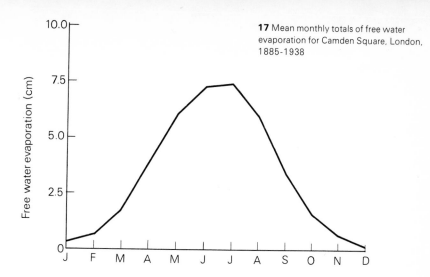

**17** Mean monthly totals of free water evaporation for Camden Square, London, 1885-1938

also have high interception rates during their growing season: 15% for maize, 7% for oats and 35% for alfalfa. The values during the dormant period fall to 3½%, 3% and 22% respectively.

The figures given above for interception loss are solely due to evaporation and do not include water that moves as stemflow to the ground surface or losses by transpiration from the plant leaves. From them it is clear that despite wide variations in the values quoted in the literature, interception is a major factor in the hydrological cycle.

## Output: the losses in the system

If the annual precipitation values for a river basin (the input values) are compared to the annual discharge from that basin (the output), it becomes apparent that there is a very considerable loss within the system. In south-east England, for example, the output is less than 30% of the input. Such estimates are calculated for natural conditions and do not include losses due to abstraction of water for industrial or domestic purposes. The difference between the input and output values on the annual scale is predominantly due to **evapotranspiration.**

Evapotranspiration is composed of two elements, namely evaporation and transpiration. **Evaporation** is the direct loss of water to the atmosphere from water, soil and other surfaces by means of physical processes. **Transpiration** is essentially a biological process, the evaporation of water from leaves of plants through openings known as **stomata**. The action of either process can be easily demonstrated but the relationship of the two processes in the field is complex, and its measurement is not easy.

### Evaporation

This can be measured by carefully observing the rate of loss from a free water surface in an open tank. Instruments of this kind are known as **evaporation pans**. There are several models but the British Standard (Meteorological Office) Sunken Evaporation Pan is one of the most satisfactory. This consists of a tank 1.8 m (6 ft) square and 61 cm (2 ft) deep sunk into the ground so that the rim projects some 8 cm (3 in) above the surrounding ground surface. The pan is equipped with a gauge to measure the water level. Readings are normally taken once a day and the change in water level noted. Clearly if any precipitation has occured between observations, allowance is

21

It is relatively simple to make and set up an evaporation pan. A large plastic washing-up bowl or baby bath is suitable. White is the best colour as less heat is absorbed, and a ruler can replace the gauge. The pan should be as large as possible, for experiments have shown that a pan of 3 m diameter gives identical values to a nearby large body of water, whilst the evaporation loss from a pan with a diameter of 1 m is exaggerated by about 20%.

made by subtracting the quantity of rainfall recorded by a rain gauge located near the tank. The tank is normally kept topped up so that the water level is some 5–10 cm below the rim. Careful note of the water used to 'top up' must be taken. Figure 17 shows mean monthly evaporation values for Camden Square in London, based on readings from 1885 to 1938.

Direct measurements of this type are of importance in assessing evaporation loss from reservoirs. Direct evaporation for the reservoir at Boulder Dam, Arizona, USA is about 150 cm per year, and for Yuma, Arizona, some 250 cm per year. The losses are so large that experiments have been conducted to attempt to reduce them by covering the water surface with a monomolecular film, similar to a film of oil; losses have been cut by 10–20%.

### Transpiration

The transpiration of a plant will vary markedly during the growing season. Before leaves emerge there is no transpiration, and as they emerge transpiration is slow. When the root structure develops the rate increases to a maximum at, or near, the flowering stage. This rate is maintained throughout the period of fruit formation and falls rapidly as the foliage begins to wither away.

Transpiration can be demonstrated by weighing a freshly cut leafy twig on a sensitive balance and observing the loss in weight as it wilts. The stomata continue to transpire but when the twig is removed from the plant there is no continuing supply of moisture. By using different plant species some relative scale of transpiration can be obtained. The problem with quantifying such work is that it is necessary to have a good estimate of the leaf area or, more precisely, of the number and size of the stomata.

### Estimates of evapotranspiration

Direct measurement of evapotranspiration over large areas is impossible but its importance in water resource planning and in agriculture has led to the development of various techniques for its estimation. On the annual scale:

EVAPOTRANSPIRATION = PRECIPITATION – RIVER RUN-OFF ± STORAGE IN THE SOIL ± GROUNDWATER LOSS

The plus or minus signs indicate that in some years evapotranspiration will draw upon the soil moisture, and possibly even groundwater, whilst in others it will not.

Studies of losses and gains within the system normally ignore the effects of groundwater loss as this is small, except where limestone or sandstone strata underlie the river basin, wholly or in part. The details of soil water storage will be considered in chapter 4 but methods of estimating the quantities are given below.

### Potential and actual evapotranspiration

At this stage it is necessary to distinguish between potential and actual evapotranspiration. **Potential evapotranspiration** can be defined as the amount of water loss that would occur if sufficient moisture were always available for the needs of the vegetation that covers the area. The real quantity is **actual evapotranspiration**, but this is so difficult to measure accurately that most evapotranspiration figures used in applied studies are estimates based upon calculations of potential evapotranspiration.

Let us illustrate this a little further. The calculated potential evapotranspiration for June in southern England is some 11 mm but precipitation is approximately 5 mm. Thus there is a June deficit of 6 mm. It is possible for the plants to draw on the store of soil moisture but this cannot continue indefinitely as the moisture stored from the winter is limited. This introduces the question of how

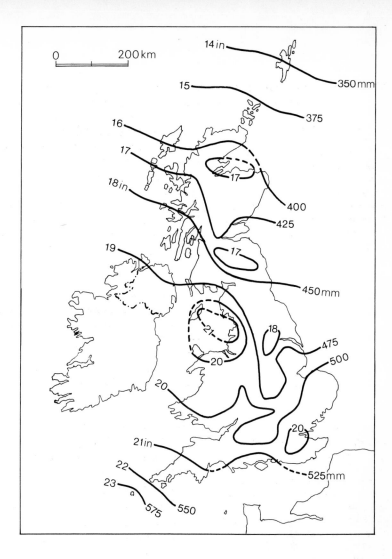

**18** Mean annual potential evapotranspiration based on the Penman formula, 1948

much soil moisture there is, or more specifically, how much soil moisture there is available to the plants.

To take a more extreme example: in a desert region it is possible to calculate the potential evapotranspiration, but this is so different from actual evapotranspiration as to be a theoretical abstraction. For example, potential evapotranspiration for Kuwait is calculated to be in excess of 350 mm for July, with an annual total of some 2100 mm, but the rainfall figures on long term averages are 0.0 mm and 13 mm respectively.

There are several methods of calculating potential evapotranspiration. These combine in various ways the meteorological factors such as sunshine hours, radiation, wind speed, turbulence, and air moisture that affect rates of evapotranspiration. Penman, an eminent British meteorologist, constructed a complex mathematical relationship for these physical processes that relied upon the data of four standard observations, namely average air temperature, average humidity, mean wind speed and the duration of bright sunshine. More sophisticated formulae require the measurement of solar radiation, and a number of special self-recording meteorological stations (often referred to as Penman stations) have been installed in various parts of Britain to obtain the data required.

23

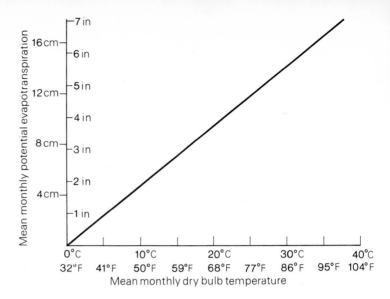

**19** Graph for the estimation of mean monthly potential evapotranspiration values from mean monthly dry bulb temperatures

A map of mean annual potential evapotranspiration values in the British Isles is given in figure 18, and clearly reflects variations in the four standard factors taken into account in the formula.

*A simplified estimate for potential evapotranspiration*
Calculations of potential evapotranspiration by the Penman method require the availability of quite sophisticated meteorological data. Rarely is this available, especially in areas of the Third World where the need for irrigation is often particularly pressing. Reasonable estimates of potential evapotranspiration can be obtained by the use of methods that only require temperature data. One such method for use in regions where the basic meteorological data are limited to dry bulb temperatures uses the formula:

$$P.E. = \frac{T - 32}{9.5}$$

where P.E. is the potential evapotranspiration in inches and T is the mean monthly temperature in degrees fahrenheit.

This relationship is graphed in figure 19, and is used to calculate the monthly potential evapotranspiration values for Patna, India, in table 4.

Table 4    *Estimates of potential evapotranspiration for Patna, India, using temperature data only*

|  | Jan. | Feb. | Mar. | Apr. | May | June | July | Aug. | Sept. | Oct. | Nov. | Dec. |
|---|---|---|---|---|---|---|---|---|---|---|---|---|
| Mean monthly dry bulb temp (°C) | 16.5 | 19.5 | 25.0 | 30.0 | 29.5 | 31.0 | 29.5 | 29.0 | 29.0 | 27.0 | 22.0 | 18.0 |
| Monthly potential evapotranspiration (cm) | 7.8 | 9.2 | 12.0 | 14.4 | 14.2 | 14.8 | 14.2 | 13.8 | 13.8 | 13.0 | 13.0 | 9.6 |

Total potential evapotranspiration = 149.8 cm

**20** The Indian sub-continent, showing
mean annual potential evapotranspiration,
precipitation and water budget

A useful exercise is to calculate the
potential evapotranspiration values
for both monthly and annual totals
and to plot the results on a map of
the area. **Isopleths** (lines on a map
through places with equal amounts
of evapotranspiration) can then be
drawn and compared to the corresponding maps of rainfall to obtain
a broad picture of the differences
between atmospheric inputs and outputs, which we shall term **water
budget**. This can be undertaken using
the basic meteorological data available from many standard textbooks.
Figure 20a illustrates the mean
annual potential evapotranspiration
figures and figure 20b the mean
annual precipitation values for a
selection of stations on the Indian
sub-continent. A further map (figure
20c) can be produced to give the
mean annual water budget.

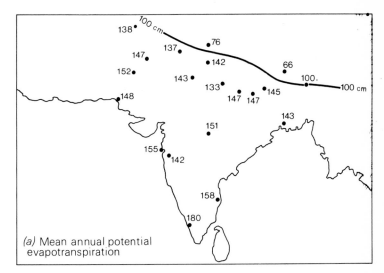

(a) Mean annual potential
evapotranspiration

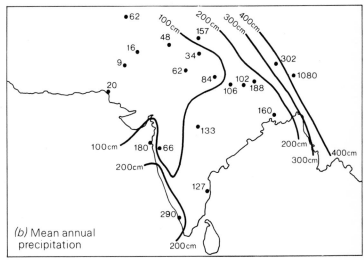

(b) Mean annual
precipitation

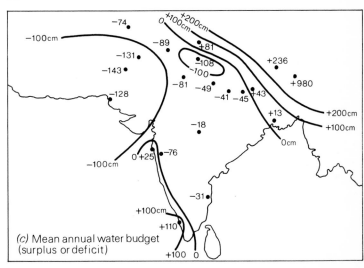

(c) Mean annual water budget
(surplus or deficit)

Table 5    *Precipitation, run-off and loss for twenty-one catchments*
*in Great Britain for the water year 1964—5*

| River basin | Precipitation in mm | Run-off in mm | Loss in mm | Run-off as a percentage of precipitation |
|---|---|---|---|---|
| 1. Eden | 1163 | 720 | 443 | 62% |
| 2. Ribble | 1302 | 995 | 307 | 76% |
| 3. Dane | 961 | 547 | 414 | 57% |
| 4. Glaslyn | 3542 | 2896 | 646 | 82% |
| 5. Ystwyth | 1563 | 1289 | 274 | 83% |
| 6. Usk | 1696 | 1219 | 477 | 72% |
| 7. Lugg | 800 | 265 | 535 | 33% |
| 8. Tone | 1017 | 375 | 642 | 37% |
| 9. Torridge | 1188 | 740 | 448 | 62% |
| 10. Itchen | 792 | 378 | 414 | 48% |
| 11. Medway | 863 | 272 | 591 | 31% |
| 12. Kennet | 704 | 153 | 551 | 22% |
| 13. Mimram | 646 | 71 | 575 | 11% |
| 14. Brett | 588 | 36 | 552 | 6% |
| 15. Yare | 739 | 132 | 607 | 18% |
| 16. Wissey | 697 | 137 | 560 | 20% |
| 17. Blithe | 809 | 251 | 558 | 31% |
| 18. Don | 911 | 352 | 559 | 39% |
| 19. Foston | 688 | 110 | 578 | 16% |
| 20. Tees | 1804 | 1049 | 755 | 58% |
| 21. Till | 858 | 370 | 488 | 43% |

*Annual rainfall and run-off figures to estimate evapotranspiration*
Comparisons of rainfall with run-off can now be made in some detail
for Great Britain as the figures, at least for the **water years** 1964—5
and 1965—6, are available in published form. These data are published
by HMSO as the *Surface Water Year Book of Great Britain*. Details
are given for some 400 stations scattered throughout Great Britain.
Two entries are reproduced in table 7 which illustrate the nature of
the information available from this source.

   Table 5 gives the precipitation (input), run-off (output), and loss
(actual evapotranspiration) for a selection of stations in England and
Wales. The information is given in terms of annual data for the water
year 1964—5, that is from i October 1964 until 30 September 1965.
The locations of the twenty-one selected stations are shown in
figure 21 and (using the data in table 5) annual precipitation for
1964—5 is plotted on figure 22 and the pattern of **isohyets** (lines
drawn on a map through places with equal rainfall) sketched in. This
demonstrates that in England and Wales there is a general decrease in
rainfall from west to east.

   If the annual figures for losses are plotted, as in figure 23, the
pattern is much less marked and it is difficult to draw isopleths for
the evapotranspiration values. However, it is clear that the variations
are much less than for precipitation. It is instructive to compare this
map to figure 18 which shows long term mean annual potential
evapotranspiration. The general pattern is of a latitudinal (north—
south) variation but with very much smaller differences than occur
for rainfall.

   A clearer illustration of the variation is to consider run-off as a
percentage of precipitation. This is shown in map form in figure 24
and as a bar graph in figure 25. There is a wide range of values and a

**21** Map showing the location of the selected river basins in table 5

**23** Map showing loss (mm) from table 5

**22** Map showing precipitation (mm) from table 5

**24** Map showing run-off as a percentage of precipitation from table 5

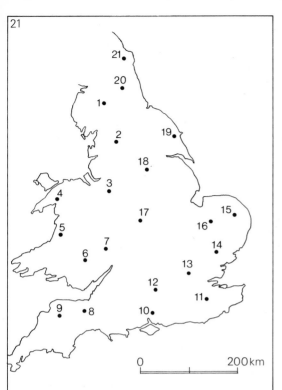

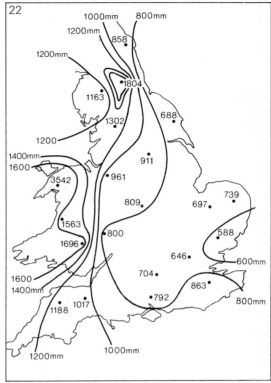

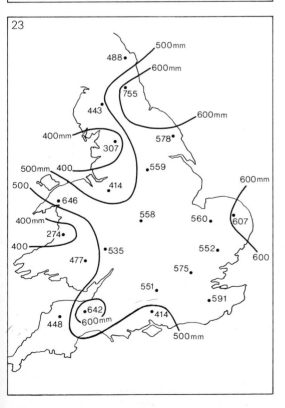

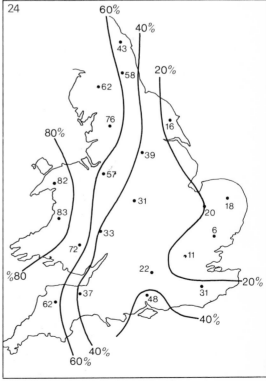

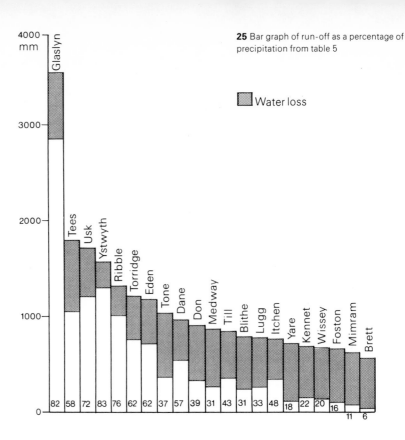

**25** Bar graph of run-off as a percentage of precipitation from table 5

clear general trend from high values in the west of the country to lower values in East Anglia and the south-east. Comparable hydrological data for the year 1965—6 is given in table 6 and can be used to make up diagrams similar to figures 22 to 25.

It must be stressed that the data for individual river gauging stations from the *Surface Water Year Book* are based upon measured river discharge and this is sometimes seriously affected by man, either withdrawing water from the river or adding effluent. However, in many cases there is a strong possibility that water that is withdrawn will be added again as effluent further downstream.

Major variations between neighbouring river basins are due to differences in geology, soil and land use of the basins. The high percentage run-off for stations in the Welsh mountains is due not only to the relatively low evapotranspiration losses but also to the fact that the catchments have only a thin cover of soil. Run-off from storms in such areas is likely to be both quick and substantial (see chapter 4); there is a similarity between the run-off from rock slopes in mountain areas to run-off from tiled roofs in urban areas. It is instructive to compare the data from various stations and to study the relevant geology, soils and land use maps to see if the effects of differences in these factors can be noticed.

*Monthly rainfall and run-off figures*
The data used so far for the British Isles have been based on annual figures where the effects of water held in storage in the soil are small. The information for individual stations in the *Surface Water Year Book* can also be used to study monthly effects. The monthly precipitation and run-off values for the River Ystwyth in Wales and the River Brett in East Anglia for the water year 1965—6 are given in table 7. The data for the River Ystwyth are plotted in figure 26 in

Evapotranspiration loss
Run–off *exceeds* precipitation

### Table 6 Precipitation, run-off and loss for twenty-one catchments for the water year 1965–6

| River basin | Precipitation in mm | Run-off in mm | Loss in mm | Run-off as a percentage of precipitation |
|---|---|---|---|---|
| 1. Eden | 1210 | 810 | 400 | 67% |
| 2. Ribble | 1518 | 1271 | 247 | 84% |
| 3. Dane | 1006 | 443 | 563 | 44% |
| 4. Glaslyn | 3503 | 2884 | 619 | 82% |
| 5. Ystwyth | 1418 | 962 | 456 | 68% |
| 6. Usk | 1534 | 1206 | 328 | 78% |
| 7. Lugg | 894 | 560 | 334 | 62% |
| 8. Tone | 1120 | 644 | 476 | 57% |
| 9. Torridge | 1252 | 926 | 326 | 74% |
| 10. Itchen | 928 | 551 | 377 | 59% |
| 11. Medway | 979 | 509 | 470 | 52% |
| 12. Kennet | 895 | 347 | 548 | 38% |
| 13. Mimram | 778 | 134 | 644 | 17% |
| 14. Brett | 573 | 163 | 410 | 28% |
| 15. Yare | 709 | 274 | 435 | 38% |
| 16. Wissey | 666 | 256 | 410 | 38% |
| 17. Blithe | 1009 | 508 | 501 | 50% |
| 18. Don | 1251 | 838 | 413 | 67% |
| 19. Foston | 904 | 648 | 256 | 72% |
| 20. Tees | 1887 | 1107 | 780 | 59% |
| 21. Till | 919 | 617 | 302 | 67% |

### Table 7 Monthly precipitation and run-off data for two catchments from the Surface Water Year Book of Great Britain, 1965–6

(a) R. Ystwyth, Wales

| 1965/66 | SOUTH WEST WALES R.A.: YSTWYTH: PONT LLOLWYN: 63/1 OCT | NOV | DEC | JAN | FEB | MAR | APR | MAY | JUN | JUL | AUG | SEP | 170 Km² YEAR |
|---|---|---|---|---|---|---|---|---|---|---|---|---|---|
| Av. gauged flow m³/s | 3.91 | 4.56 | 22.59 | 4.62 | 6.86 | 3.11 | 2.87 | 2.99 | 3.98 | 2.07 | 2.36 | 2.25 | 5.19 |
| Av. gross flow m³/s | 3.91 | 4.56 | 22.59 | 4.62 | 6.86 | 3.11 | 2.87 | 2.99 | 3.98 | 2.07 | 2.36 | 2.25 | 5.19 |
| Av. unit gross flow l/s Km² | 23.01 | 26.83 | 132.86 | 27.20 | 40.32 | 18.27 | 16.88 | 17.60 | 23.44 | 12.16 | 13.88 | 13.22 | 30.51 |
| Run-off mm | 62 | 70 | 356 | 73 | 98 | 49 | 44 | 47 | 61 | 33 | 37 | 34 | 962 |
| Rainfall mm | 76 | 122 | 341 | 64 | 149 | 80 | 85 | 109 | 127 | 115 | 60 | 90 | 1418 |
| Rainfall–Run-off mm | 14 | 52 | −15 | −9 | 51 | 31 | 41 | 62 | 66 | 82 | 23 | 56 | 456 |
| Highest gauged flow m³/s | 35.09 | 21.62 | 151.40 | 29.43 | 32.83 | 16.73 | 18.82 | 25.92 | 110.37 | 13.39 | 11.77 | 42.45 | 151.40 |
| Max. dly. gauged flow m³/s | 20.35 | 15.11 | 98.20 | 17.72 | 17.55 | 11.09 | 11.97 | 13.75 | 49.81 | 6.59 | 8.49 | 9.71 | 98.20 |
| Min. dly. gauged flow m³/s | 0.96 | 1.78 | 4.08 | 1.37 | 2.15 | 0.96 | 0.85 | 1.08 | 0.93 | 0.74 | 0.79 | 0.59 | 0.59 |

(b) R. Brett, East Anglia

| 1965/66 | ESSEX R.A.: BRETT: HADLEIGH MILL: 36/5 OCT | NOV | DEC | JAN | FEB | MAR | APR | MAY | JUN | JUL | AUG | SEP | 156 Km² YEAR |
|---|---|---|---|---|---|---|---|---|---|---|---|---|---|
| Av. gauged flow m³/s | 0.28 | 0.72 | 3.24 | 1.29 | 1.73 | 0.51 | 0.93 | 0.35 | 0.21 | 0.19 | 0.16 | 0.13 | 0.81 |
| Av. gross flow m³/s | 0.28 | 0.72 | 3.24 | 1.29 | 1.73 | 0.51 | 0.93 | 0.35 | 0.21 | 0.19 | 0.16 | 0.13 | 0.81 |
| Av. unit gross flow l/s Km² | 1.77 | 4.63 | 20.75 | 8.27 | 11.06 | 3.29 | 5.97 | 2.25 | 1.35 | 1.22 | 1.00 | 0.81 | 5.17 |
| Run-off mm | 5 | 12 | 56 | 22 | 27 | 9 | 15 | 6 | 3 | 3 | 3 | 2 | 163 |
| Rainfall mm | 15 | 60 | 99 | 28 | 48 | 14 | 54 | 42 | 47 | 89 | 55 | 22 | 573 |
| Rainfall–Run-off mm | 10 | 48 | 43 | 6 | 21 | 5 | 39 | 36 | 44 | 86 | 52 | 20 | 410 |
| Highest gauged flow m³/s | 2.67 | 6.28 | 12.03 | 4.47 | 5.94 | 1.50 | 5.38 | 0.62 | 0.35 | 0.55 | 0.37 | 0.34 | 12.03 |
| Max. dly. gauged flow m³/s | 2.17 | 5.18 | 10.61 | 3.71 | 4.92 | 1.17 | 4.33 | 0.56 | 0.30 | 0.50 | 0.32 | 0.22 | 10.61 |
| Min. dly. gauged flow m³/s | 0.11 | 0.07 | 0.87 | 0.47 | 0.69 | 0.31 | 0.31 | 0.25 | 0.18 | 0.12 | 0.11 | 0.10 | 0.07 |

the form of a bar graph with the loss shaded. This shows that in two of the winter months the run-off actually exceeds the precipitation, which means that water must be drawn from storage. It is also apparent that the evapotranspiration losses are greater in the summer than in the winter. The same effect is observed if the data for the River Brett are plotted.

Table 8 gives the calculated mean monthly potential evapotranspi-

29

ration and the monthly precipitation for Lincoln, England. It can be seen that for the winter months there is a surplus of precipitation over evapotranspiration. This surplus either recharges the store of soil moisture or becomes run-off. In the summer, when evapotranspiration is in excess of precipitation, the plants draw on the store of soil moisture.

## The soil moisture store and irrigation

It is necessary at this stage to discuss two further terms, field capacity and wilting point. **Field capacity** is the maximum quantity of water that the soil can retain against the force of gravity. Any further addition of water drains rapidly from the soil (see figure 35). **Wilting point** is simply the stage at which the plants obtain no further moisture from the soil and start to wilt. It must be stressed that moisture is still present in the soil when the wilting point is reached but is no longer available to the plants. The moisture retained at wilting point is so closely held by the soil particles that the 'suction' effects exerted by the plant roots cannot overcome the soil factors that act to retain the water. Both field capacity and wilting point vary, even at the local scale. The field capacity for clays is greater than that for sands, and similarly wilting point is higher for clays than for sands. Chapter 4 looks at this further.

It is difficult to define exactly the wilting point for a given plant species at a particular location. However, a relative scale can be obtained by considering the depth of rooting of various plants. The deeper the root penetration the greater the soil water store that can be tapped at times of moisture deficit. A table of rooting depths applicable to crops in deep, free-draining fertile soils is given in table 9.

A further problem is that as the soil moisture store becomes depleted the actual evapotranspiration will become considerably less than the potential evapotranspiration. In other words the plant transpiration becomes reduced and growth is adversely affected. The moisture deficit at which this occurs is known as the **root constant**. Figures are available that give approximate values for the root constant for different crops and these are shown in table 10. They give an indication of when the moisture deficits start to limit agricultural production. Such information is crucial for an understanding of irrigation needs, although the detailed planning of irrigation for a specific region is best based upon actual field experiments. However,

Table 8    *Precipitation and potential evapotranspiration data for Lincoln (mm)*

|  | Oct. | Nov. | Dec. | Jan. | Feb. | Mar. | Apr. | May | June | July | Aug. | Sept. |
|---|---|---|---|---|---|---|---|---|---|---|---|---|
| Precipitation (for Oct. 1965–Sept. 1966) | 11 | 88 | 124 | 40 | 87 | 21 | 81 | 47 | 72 | 62 | 90 | 27 |
| Mean potential evapotranspiration | 22 | 5 | 1 | 2 | 10 | 32 | 55 | 84 | 94 | 93 | 76 | 50 |
| Surplus or deficit (−) of precipitation over evapotranspiration | −11 | 83 | 123 | 38 | 77 | −11 | 26 | −37 | −22 | −31 | 14 | −23 |

for the initial planning the establishment of the overall water budget is based on the principles outlined above.

Irrigation is clearly essential for crop production in arid regions but can also be of importance in more humid climates. For example, grass yields in Britain can be increased by over 100% by judicious irrigation in years with a dry summer, and by perhaps 50% when rainfall conditions are average. The areas where irrigation is of particular importance and economic value are in the south-east of England and in East Anglia. In these areas irrigation would be beneficial in about nine years out of ten. Irrigation of the spray type is not only used to increase grass production but considerable acreages of potatoes and sugar beet are also irrigated with worthwhile increases in yield.

Table 9    *Typical rooting depths for various crops*

| Crop | Depth | Crop | Depth |
|------|-------|------|-------|
| Alfalfa | 2–3 m | Deciduous orchards | 2–3 m |
| Artichokes | 1–3 m | Grain | 1.3 m |
| Asparagus | 2–3 m | Grass pasture | 1 m |
| Beans | 1 m | Clover | up to 1 m |
| Beets (sugar) | 1.3–2 m | Lettuce | up to 0.3 m |
| Beets (table) | up to 1 m | Onions | up to 0.3 m |
| Broccoli | 0.7 m | Parsnips | 1 m |
| Cabbage | 0.7 m | Peas | 1–1.3 m |
| Carrots | up to 1 m | Potatoes | 1–1.3 m |
| Cauliflower | up to 1 m | Potatoes (sweet) | 1.3–2 m |
| Citrus | 1.3–2 m | Tomatoes | 2 m |
| Corn (sweet) | 1 m | Turnips | 1 m |
| Corn (field) | 1 m | Strawberries | 1 m |
| Cotton | up to 2 m | Watermelons | 2 m |

Table 10    *Root constants of common crops*

| Crops | Root constant (mm) |
|-------|--------------------|
| Cereals | 200 |
| Potatoes | 150 |
| Beans and peas | 100 |
| Turnips, swedes and fodder beet | 150 |
| Cabbage, savoys and kale | 125 |
| Sugar beet | 150 |
| Hops | 200 |
| Orchards, grown commercially | 225 |
| Orchards, not grown commercially | 200 |
| Vegetables, nursery plants | 100 |
| Lucerne | 150 |
| Clover, sainfoin | 100 |
| Temporary grasses | 100 |
| Permanent grasses | 125 |
| Rough grazing | 50 |
| Permanent woodland | 250 (125 on poor land) |

## Soil moisture and river flow

At times when a soil moisture deficit exists, e.g. for the months of May, June and July in Lincoln as shown in table 8, river flow still continues. The reasons for this are several. First, some portion of the river discharge is often drawn from groundwater which is a separate store in the hydrological system. Second, parts of the river basin with differing soil conditions have different field capacities. Third, the method of measurement provides an estimate which does not completely match natural conditions; there is an error term. But most important, we have been using monthly average figures. The most likely situation is that during summer there would be some rain, soil moisture would be recharged, and this would then be followed by a dry period with considerable evapotranspiration loss. In other words monthly figures are not sufficiently detailed. It is possible to apply the same budget principles to daily data with better results.

The Meteorological Office in Britain has recognised the need for information on soil moisture conditions and publishes maps illustrating the state of soil moisture deficits at intervals throughout the year. These are relatively expensive but are used by River Authorities, farmers and water engineers as a guide to the prevailing situation.

The value of water budget studies of this kind in agriculture is evident, but such studies are also of importance for flood warnings. If an area has a large soil moisture deficit it can absorb a large proportion of the rain that falls. Thus a heavy period of rain of, say, 100 mm in two days, presents a real flood hazard when the soils are already at field capacity but no flood hazard when the soil has a water deficit that may be 80 mm. In addition to flood hazards, soil moisture deficits of this kind are of practical importance to reservoir storage. After a period of summer drought and possible rural shortages of water for domestic and industrial use the first rains do little to alleviate the water supply problem, frequently to the annoyance of the users who consider that if it has rained their drought-stricken water supplies should immediately return to normal!

In this chapter we have looked at the balance particularly between inputs of precipitation and losses due to evapotranspiration in the river basin, since these clearly affect the other output which concerns us, that of run-off. Some attention has already been given to soil moisture and in the next chapter this will be examined further in an attempt to understand more about the black box area of figure 12. In particular we shall look at the time lag between precipitation and the response to it in the river channel.

## Selected references

HMSO. 1966. *The Surface Water Year Book of Great Britain, 1964–5.* London.

HMSO. 1971. *The Surface Water Year Book of Great Britain, 1965–6.* London.

Meteorological Office. Annual. *British Rainfall.* London: HMSO.

MAFF. 1976. *Technical Bulletin 34 Climate and Drainage.* London: HMSO.

Penman, H.L. 1963. Vegetation and hydrology. *Technical Communication,* no. 53. Commonwealth Agricultural Bureau.

# 4

# Water movement through soil

Chapter 3 showed how the discharge of a river is affected by both the intensity and the distribution of precipitation, and how these effects are modified by interception and evapotranspiration losses and by storage in the soil before the water reaches a river channel.

Although some precipitation falls directly into the river channels themselves, their area is but a small proportion of the total basin area. Direct channel precipitation is, therefore, small though nevertheless important for its immediate effect. Most precipitation falls on surrounding land, and therefore has a journey to make before reaching the stream channel — it is this journey that we consider here.

It was long assumed that water springing from the ground came either from the Earth's interior or was somehow returned underground from the sea's plentiful stocks. It was not until 1674 that a Frenchman, Pierre Perrault, measured rainfall and run-off in the Paris Basin and found rain to be a more than adequate supply. As shown in figure 12, the black box diagram, it is known that the

**27** Downslope routes for water

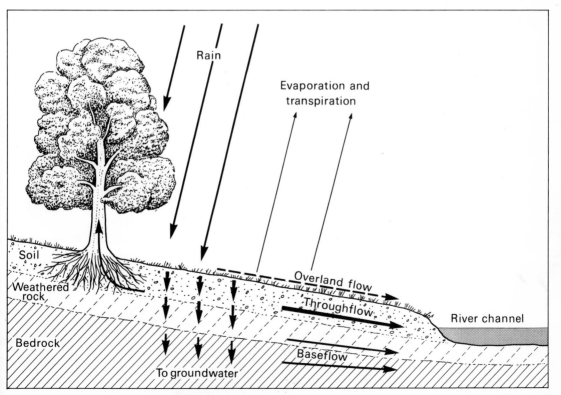

**28** Precipitation (represented by bar graph) and run-off (represented by line graph) for R. Browney, Co. Durham, England, January and June 1971

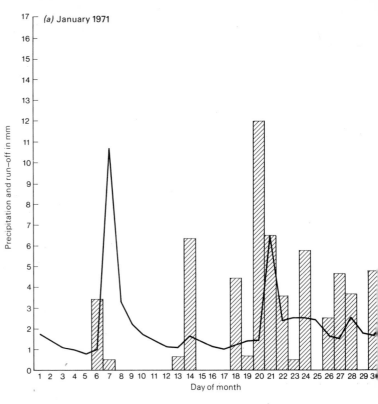

(a) January 1971

Precipitation and run—off in mm

Day of month

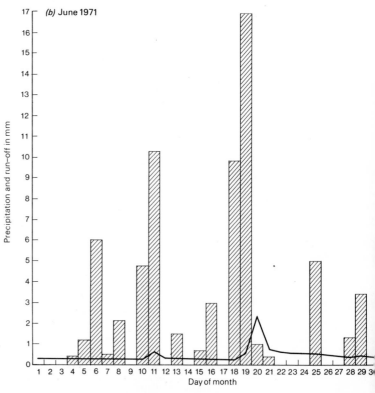

(b) June 1971

Precipitation and run-off in mm

Day of month

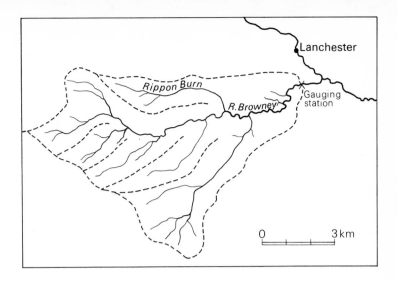

**29** Basin of R. Browney, Co. Durham, England

input of effective precipitation (that is, precipitation less interception and evapotranspiration) is the sole source of the output of river discharge. What happens in between input and output is not known. The aim of this chapter is to attempt to add detail within the black box.

Until recently, many assumptions were made about how precipitation onto a hillslope eventually reached a river channel, assumptions which have needed considerable modification. Figure 27 shows possible routes the water may take downslope. One obvious route is over the land surface, termed **overland flow**, another is to seep downhill in the soil layers, **throughflow** or **interflow**, and a third is very slow seepage via soil and bedrock, termed **baseflow**. That from bedrock alone is called **groundwater flow**. Obviously the extent to which any of these routes is used will vary from basin to basin, depending upon such factors as rock permeability, soil texture and depth, and rainfall intensity in particular.

## Input—output time lag

Figure 28 shows daily rainfall and run-off for the River Browney in Co. Durham, England for two months in 1971. Comparison of the peaks in each month reveals that there is a time lag between the occurrence of rainfall in the basin and the time when that water passes the gauging station near Lanchester. In most instances this lag seems to be approximately one day — for example, the peak rainfall on 6 January produces a peak run-off on 7 January. Thus there is a need to account for a twenty-four hour delay.

Crude calculations can easily be made to indicate the time spent moving downstream in this catchment if figure 29 is used. The average distance of water flow to the gauging station is given approximately by the mean channel length, as described in chapter 5. This amounts to 11.26 km. The mean velocity of water at the gauging station is 5.2 km/hr.

Assuming this velocity for the whole channel length, the water therefore takes, very roughly, two hours to move along the river channel. Despite the numerous approximations made here, this channel movement accounts for only a small part of the lag between rainfall and discharge peaks. It leaves about twenty-two hours to be accounted for by downslope movement of water towards the stream channel.

35

The average distance, measured from the map, between watershed and channel is approximately 500 m. Halving this will give an approximation for the average distance downslope that water has to travel — 250 m. Thus the water would only need to travel at a speed of 12.5 m/hr (20 cm/minute) in order to cover this distance in the twenty-two hours available.

In fact, the rate of flow of the water over the ground surface will be nearer to that in the channel itself. Allowing for the greater roughness of the ground surface, and the lesser depth of water for overland flow compared with channel flow, we can assume that the overland flow rate will be about one tenth of the channel flow rate. This gives an approximate overland flow rate of 0.15 m/sec (900 cm/minute) which is still forty-five times faster than the downhill movement we have calculated actually takes place. It is unlikely therefore that overland flow contributes much, if anything, to peak flows.

Groundwater movement rates are known to range from 150 cm/yr to 150 cm/day depending upon the permeability of the bedrock. In the catchment under consideration the bedrock is mostly composed of Coal Measures, which is almost impermeable, or of very low permeability. Groundwater flows, an important part of baseflow, are therefore very slow and probably contribute little to peak discharges of the River Browney.

Throughflow, the movement of water downslope via soil layers, is thus the most likely dominant contributor to river discharge. This is highly plausible but had been barely recognised until very recently in most geographical and even hydrological textbooks. Yet it is the dominant route for most run-off in temperate latitudes. Groundwater flow becomes important only on permeable rocks, and overland flow occurs to any extent only with heavy rainfalls onto saturated or shallow soils.

It is possible, therefore, to deduce theoretically the dominant route which moisture takes downslope. It is necessary however to examine recent experimental measurements to see if they corroborate these deductions and if they can throw further light upon the controls governing which route is selected.

## Field and experimental measurements

Measurements of the contribution of overland flow, throughflow and, by deduction, groundwater flow can be made in the field by opening up a pit on a hillside and installing gutters to collect water from different soil layers. This is described more fully in Gregory and Walling (1973). Measurements by Weyman on brown earth soils and peaty podsols overlying virtually impermeable bedrock of Old Red Sandstone on slopes of twelve degrees in Somerset, England are given in table 11. Both the soils are shown to be divided into different layers, or **horizons**, with differing organic contents, textures and structures. The figures for the brown earth soils show that twenty-four hours elapsed between the peak rainfall and peak flow from the B-horizon in the soil. Drainage from this horizon continued for up to five days following rainfall whilst that from the B/C-horizon continued for more than forty days, peaking five to six days after rainfall. Throughflow drainage did not occur in the topmost soil horizon and neither

**Table 11** *Throughflow rates on a 12° slope in an upland catchment in Somerset*

| | Soil horizon | | Bulk density | Flows | Lag of storm peak | Drainage time |
|---|---|---|---|---|---|---|
| *Brown earth soil* | A | 0–10 cm (organic) | – | – | – | – |
| | B | 10–45 cm (sandy loam) | 1.6 g/cm³ – 1.9 g/cm³ | 0–180 cm³/min | 24 hrs | 5 days |
| | B/C | 45–75 cm | – | 1–10 cm³/min | 5–6 days | > 40 days |
| *Peaty podsols* | A | 0–20 cm (peat) | – | – | 2–3 hrs via 5 cm pipes at 20 cm depth | – |
| | B | 20–60 cm (podsol) | – | – | – | – |

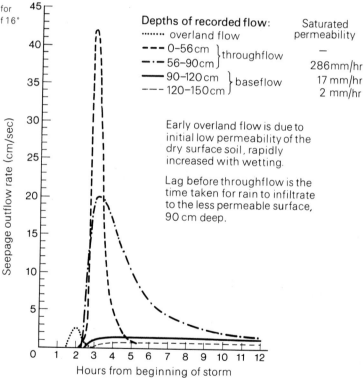

**30** Discharges from flow within soil for storm of 2 hrs, 5·1 cm/hr, on slope of 16° (drained for 4 days prior)

Seepage outflow rate (cm/sec)

Hours from beginning of storm

Depths of recorded flow:     Saturated permeability

········ overland flow     –

– – – 0–56 cm ⎱ throughflow     286 mm/hr
–·– 56–90 cm ⎰

—— 90–120 cm ⎱ baseflow     17 mm/hr
– – – 120–150 cm ⎰     2 mm/hr

Early overland flow is due to initial low permeability of the dry surface soil, rapidly increased with wetting.

Lag before throughflow is the time taken for rain to infiltrate to the less permeable surface, 90 cm deep.

did overland flow. What is more, the slow flow from the B/C-horizon was sufficient to maintain continuous streamflow throughout the year, that is to say it maintained a 'baseflow' similar to that which would be provided by groundwater from permeable rocks.

The discharge from flow within a soil for a heavy storm was calculated from field measurements of throughflow rates by Whipkey, the American hydrologist, to produce the **storm hydrograph** in figure 30. This clearly illustrates the theoretical contribution of dif-

37

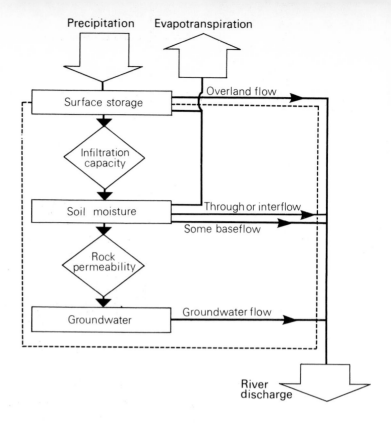

ferent soil horizons (and therefore rates of flow) to the total discharge, in particular the difference in the relative peaks of throughflow discharge and baseflow from the lowest horizons. The latter
rises slowly and is maintained for a much longer period. The relative
contribution of each obviously has an important effect upon stream
discharge characteristics. Dominance of the higher horizons produces
rapid changes in discharge compared to the more steady flows
derived from lower horizons.

These two brief examples support the deduction of the important
contribution of flow through soil horizons to stream discharges.
Clearly the relative importance of different routes will depend
broadly upon whether the soil can absorb rainfall as fast as it falls,
and whether the bedrock can absorb percolating water as fast as it
sinks down through the soil horizons. The rates of water absorption
at these two surfaces — soil and bedrock — act as **regulators** controlling which route is selected. This is illustrated in figure 31 which
should be compared with the original black box diagram (figure 12).

## Regulators

The regulators — the infiltration rate into soil and the permeability
of bedrock — indicated in figure 31 by diamond-shaped symbols,
will now be examined in turn, followed by examination of storage
zones — surface, soil and bedrock.

### Infiltration rates

A block of soil can be compared very simply to a tin can with a fine
wire gauze over its top. Water poured onto its surface will only overflow either if the water is poured at a rate faster than the gauze will
allow it through, or when sufficient water has been poured to fill the
can so that it can hold no more. Although this is an oversimplification
it illustrates the two factors that hold water upon the ground surface:

Relative infiltration rates for different soil types can be measured fairly easily using the following method (see figure 32). A bottomless container 20 cm in diameter is sunk 10 cm into the ground. It is then filled with water to a level 15 cm above the ground. The time that the water level takes to fall 5 cm is recorded. The experiment should be repeated until the times taken are roughly constant for three successive repeats. The results are given in mm/sec by dividing the difference in levels (50 mm) by the time taken.

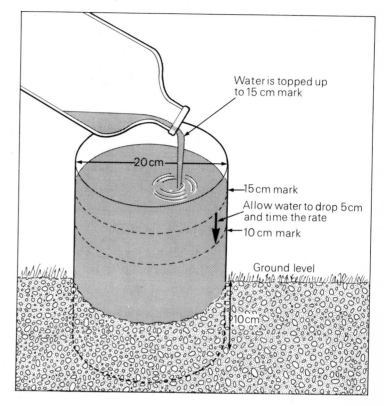

Water is topped up to 15 cm mark

20 cm

15 cm mark

Allow water to drop 5 cm and time the rate

10 cm mark

Ground level

10 cm

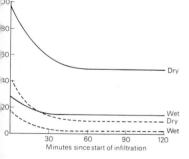

Dry

Wet
Dry
Wet

30    60    90    120
Minutes since start of infiltration

**33** Infiltration curves, showing wet and dry conditions in a sandy loam (solid line) and a clay loam (broken line)

(1) the rate at which the ground surface can absorb water, its **infiltration rate**, and (2) the capacity of the soil for holding water, its field capacity (see chapter 3).

Calculation of the likelihood of surface, or overland flow, thus requires measurement of rainfall intensities and of infiltration capacities of the soil. Average rainfall intensity for a storm can of course be measured from recording rain gauges. Averages range in temperate latitudes from less than 2 mm/hr in light rain to 7 to over 10 mm/hr for heavy rain. Very rare storms, such as that which produced floods in the Mendip Hills, Somerset, England, in 1968, may however, reach maximum intensities of as much as 70 mm/hr, but even these do not often exceed the infiltration capacities of soils. Most published data record daily rainfall rather than individual storms, so specific measurements of storm intensities generally have to be made for use in hydrological studies.

Figure 33 shows typical infiltration rates for two soils, and also illustrates the effect of existing soil moisture conditions on infiltration rates; note that wet soils have slower rates. It demonstrates the importance of taking readings on the same day if they are to be used for comparison of the effects of soil, slope, etc. on infiltration rates.

These measurements will not of course indicate specific rates of rainfall infiltration. More sophisticated instrumentation is required to simulate raindrop seepage. But the measurements do provide effective means of comparing rates for different soil types, on trodden and untrodden areas of the same soil, or on areas with surface litter and without.

One important characteristic of infiltration is its decline from a high rate to a steady level. It is this steady level, reached after anything from several minutes to an hour, which is given as the **infiltration capacity** or **saturated infiltration rate** for a soil. The fall in the rate as the soil becomes wet indicates the importance of the moisture content of the soil before the rainfall begins. If it is already moist the low steady rate is more quickly achieved and overland flow is more likely to occur. Similarly, the duration of a storm is of importance. The initial high infiltration rates into a dry soil may allow absorption of quite intense rainfall. But as the infiltration rate declines it may fall below the rainfall intensity, and in this case too overland flow is likely to occur.

Measurements of infiltration rates show a considerable range of values, from about 2 mm/hr on bare clays to 12 mm/hr on bare sands. But considerably higher rates are shown on vegetated ground, as indicated in table 12, which also illustrates a decrease in rate on ground trampled by heavy grazing. In general, however, the figures suggest that for all but the heaviest rainfalls in the British Isles and in similar climates, most soils can absorb the precipitation as it falls, hence the limited occurrence, suggested earlier, of overland flow.

*Bedrock permeability*
Whether or not groundwater flow makes a significant contribution to stream discharge depends upon the **permeability** of the underlying bedrock in a basin. Permeability in a rock is a measurement of the rate of flow of water through it. This may occur through primary pores that exist between the grains of rock, especially in unconsolidated (i.e. non-cemented) sediments, or through secondary cracks of various kinds in rocks, as illustrated in figure 34. The larger its pores or cracks, in general, the more permeable is a rock. 'Primary' permeability will not vary much from one part of the rock to another, while 'secondary' permeability will vary from place to place according to the presence or absence and size of cracks.

A significant percentage of the volume of all unconsolidated sedimentary deposits is occupied by pore spaces and so these rocks (gravels, sands and silts) are quite permeable, except for clays in which the pore spaces, though numerous, are too small to allow water easily to pass through. Values of primary permeability may

Table 12    *Influence of ground cover on infiltration rates (for Cecil, Madison and Durham soils)*

| Ground cover | Infiltration rates (mm/hr) |
| --- | --- |
| Old permanent pasture | 57 |
| Permanent pasture: moderately grazed | 19 |
| Permanent pasture: heavily grazed | 13 |
| Strip-cropped | 10 |
| Weeds or grain | 9 |
| Clean tilled | 7 |
| Bare, crusted ground | 6 |

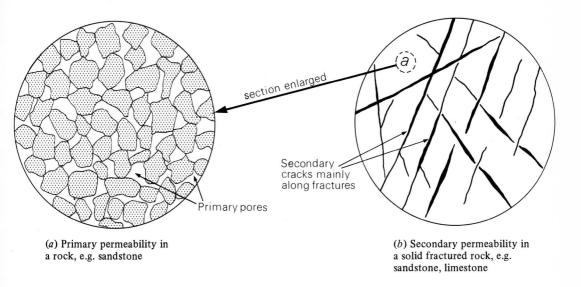

(*a*) Primary permeability in
a rock, e.g. sandstone

(*b*) Secondary permeability in
a solid fractured rock, e.g.
sandstone, limestone

range from 20 000 cm/hr for gravels to 10 cm/hr for silts. As these
sediments become more consolidated, e.g. to form conglomerates,
sandstones or siltstones, their porosity decreases. Their primary
permeability also decreases, from 200 cm/hr in some sandstones to
virtually zero in well-consolidated sediments.

A very rough generalisation can be made that the older a rock is
the more likely it is to have been consolidated. For example in
Britain the Old Red Sandstone (400 million years old) is so well
consolidated that it has almost lost its primary permeability, whilst
New Red Sandstone outcrops of Bunter Sandstone and Keuper Marls
(270 million years old) are relatively permeable and the Lower and
Upper Greensand of the Weald of Kent (140 million years old) are
even more permeable. But older rocks are more likely to be crushed
and cracked and therefore to have developed a secondary
permeability.

The secondary permeability of fissured rocks, which include the
major limestone outcrops of Chalk, Jurassic Limestone and Carboniferous Limestone, is much more difficult to measure. Chalk, being
very highly fissured, and Jurassic Limestone, being very sandy as
well as fissured, behave very similarly to porous rocks, apart from
local variations due to differing degrees of fissuring. In Carboniferous
Limestone the degree of fissuring controls permeability completely
since the rock itself has virtually no pore spaces. Nevertheless,
Carboniferous Limestone is frequently so well criss-crossed by joints
and bedding-planes (many of which have become enlarged in time
by solution and often form systems of open cave passages) that flow
through the rock is quite rapid. One calculation for the Cheddar area
of Somerset, England gives an average flow rate in large fissures for
the basin of 583 cm/hr. It is hardly surprising that on this rock in
this basin there is no surface drainage at all.

In general, then, limestones and less well consolidated sandstones
and coarser sediments are likely to have permeabilities that are
higher than rainfall intensities. Therefore the bedrock absorbs rainfall as groundwater which reappears as springs. On consolidated

41

sandstones and other well-jointed rocks, such as basalts, the permeability of the bedrock may be sufficient to allow some percolation of groundwater but a proportion of precipitation will also flow downslope through the soil layers. Similarly, most clays and shales have such low permeabilities that for our purposes they may be regarded as impermeable.

## Storage zones
Referring back to figure 31, attention now needs to be focussed upon the storage boxes and the flows through them.

*Surface storage and overland flow*
It has been indicated that water will lie on the ground surface either when rainfall intensity exceeds infiltration rates, or when the soil becomes saturated so that it is unable to hold further supplies of water. Rain water that cannot infiltrate does not automatically produce overland flow since there will always be some surface irregularity to collect water in puddles. Such surface storage, of course, varies according to the irregularity of the ground surface. Deliberate use is made of this effect in contour ploughing to retain surface moisture and inhibit overland flow.

Surface storage is of course a relatively small component of the total storage, compared with soil moisture storage. Water collected on the surface may eventually infiltrate into the ground or be lost through evaporation.

Surface water, more frequently the result of saturation of the soil following prolonged rainfall, may occur in upland areas where impermeable bedrock, shallow soils and frequent rain produce conditions conducive to overland flow. Such flow commonly occurs evenly over hillsides in poorly vegetated semi-arid areas and is termed **sheetwash**. In such areas its erosive powers are quite considerable but densely vegetated hillslopes are less likely to suffer such erosion. Nevertheless, considerable erosion, commonly causing gullying, does occur occasionally when heavy storms fall upon newly ploughed land, particularly if the ploughlines run downslope.

In lowland areas of Britain surface water is generally the result of a combination of heavy or prolonged rainfall and the concentration of throughflow seepage in hollows and at the base of slopes. Clearly, locally infiltrated water combined with water seeping down from upslope may saturate the soil where slopes flatten out.

*Soil moisture*
The analogy of a gauze-covered tin can, used to illustrate the limiting conditions when overland flow might occur, can be adapted and refined further to illustrate soil moisture conditions as in figure 35. The surface gauze still represents the limiting infiltration capacity of the soil surface but now two types of outlet are included — one representing soakage into a permeable bedrock and several representing downslope movement of water by throughflow. Water poured onto the can will filter through the gauze and fill it until it rises to the level of the outflow when it will begin to flow out, to sink down pipe b, and, if the supply is great enough, to overflow along pipe a as

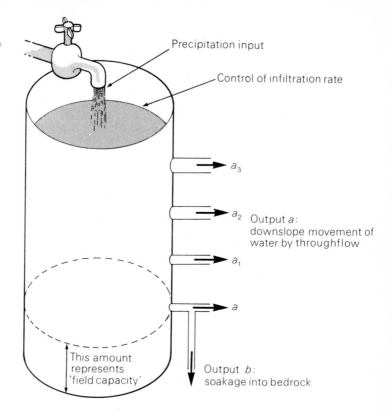

**35** Model representation of soil moisture characteristics

Precipitation input

Control of infiltration rate

$a_3$

$a_2$ Output *a*: downslope movement of water by throughflow

$a_1$

*a*

This amount represents 'field capacity'

Output *b*: soakage into bedrock

throughflow. If the water supply rate is greater than these two pipes can remove, the water level will rise up the can and flow out of the various horizons, at ever faster rates. If the supply continues for long enough and fast enough, it may eventually flow over the top, representing surface flow.

This analogy is an oversimplification since some downslope movement of water will occur before field capacity is reached. However, it serves to illustrate some of the important characteristics of soil moisture. The first is that water added to a dry soil will not soak out from its base until a certain moisture level in the soil is reached. This level is the soil's field capacity and it represents water held by capillary tension in the soil pore spaces.

Some values of field capacities are given in table 13, which reveals an increase with decreasing grain, and therefore pore, size. Grain size, though important, is not the sole determinant of field capacity level since packing and humus content will also affect pore size. Soil pores are of two types – capillary pores (less than 0.075 mm diameter) which retain moisture, and larger non-capillary pores which allow

---

Field capacity can be demonstrated by taking a sample of soil (as little disturbed as possible) and drying it (at 80–100°C for twenty-four hours). Then, holding it over a close-meshed sieve, gently pour a known quantity of water onto its surface, collecting whatever drains through. Comparison of the amount which drains through with the known quantity poured onto the surface will give the volume retained in the soil which is now at its field capacity. The moisture content can be represented by expressing the volume of water retained in the soil as a percentage of the volume of soil used for the experiment.

Table 13  *The amount of water held against the pull of gravity in cm/m of the soil profile*

| Soil type | Water held (cm/m) |
|---|---|
| Sand and loamy sands | 2–4 |
| Sandy loams | 8 |
| Fine sandy loams | 12–14 |
| Loams | 17 |
| Clay loams | 25 |
| Clays | 29 |

water to drain through. The field capacity of a soil is related to the proportion of capillary pores, and its permeability is related to the proportion of larger pore spaces. Both are important characteristics of a soil. Capillary moisture is drawn upon by plants, and the larger pores aerate the soil enabling important bacterial and other organic processes to change the nutrients supplied by humus and weathered bedrock into forms which plants can use.

Field capacity is a useful measurement, representing the maximum moisture content of the soil under free drainage. If moisture surplus to field capacity is held in the soil, it is held in the non-capillary pores and so reduces aeration of the soil. Soils in which this occurs are characterised by grey tones often with blotchy orange or yellow patches of oxidation. They are termed **gleys** and require artificial drainage to improve them for cultivation.

Humus is an important agent in the soil because it links clay particles together into **crumbs** which have fine capillary pores within them yet allow water to drain between them. Soils with less than 3% organic matter may be structurally unstable. Good arable soils may have between 5 and 8% organic matter.

Other important soil structures which affect drainage are shown in figure 36. Vertical fissuring and blocky or granular structures (**peds**) promote vertical drainage, whereas **platy** structures impede it. Platy structures are common when wet soils are packed down, or 'poached', for example by machinery or trampling or ploughing when wet.

Vertical drainage may be further impeded through deposition, especially in coarse textured soils, of salts leached from the top layers. Iron is most commonly involved and deposition of iron salts can build up an impermeable, hard 'iron-pan' layer which can give rise to the anomalous situation of impeded drainage upon sandy soils.

It is clear that the assumption of only two limiting factors (infiltration and bedrock impermeability) controlling flow routes is too simple. Additional controlling structures undoubtedly exist in many soils to direct drainage through particular levels within them. Such flows, however, at whatever level and at whatever rate of flow, may be grouped together as throughflow.

*Throughflow*
Study of throughflow is still in its early stages but some indications can be given of its character and variations. The hydrographs in figure 30 reveal that differences in rates of flow in different soil horizons may be quite considerable, imparting as they do here quite different discharge characteristics. Rapid flow in the upper horizons produced strongly peaked discharges whilst that from lower horizons

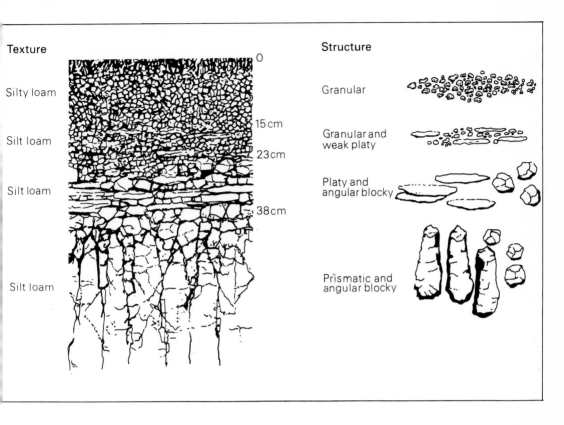

Texture

Silty loam

Silt loam

Silt loam

Silt loam

O

15 cm

23 cm

38 cm

Structure

Granular

Granular and weak platy

Platy and angular blocky

Prismatic and angular blocky

was slow and prolonged. The latter kind of flow is similar to groundwater flow and is generally included with it under the category of baseflow. The results presented in table 11 confirm that baseflow can be produced from such soil water movement, as distinct from groundwater flow through underlying permeable rock. Rates of flow will naturally depend upon such factors as soil texture, soil structure and the gradient of the slope on which the soils occur. The routes also vary, however, according to the degree and manner of concentration of flow paths through the soils. Two types of flow path have been observed in the field.

Table 11 shows that in the one upland catchment there are two soil types: brown earths and peaty podsols. We have already considered the flow rates through the former soils, but the table shows that flow rates through the latter rose to a peak ten times more quickly than on the brown earths. This more rapid flow is due to the development of small **pipes** up to 5 cm in diameter near the base of the peat. Such pipes, illustrated in figure 37, have been quite widely observed on most soil types, commonly within the B-horizons of soils, and develop naturally from cracks, worm and animal burrows, and root holes. The size of the pipe illustrated can be gauged by the film carton beside it, but they have been observed to reach considerable sizes, several feet across, in New Zealand and Canada for example. Flows are naturally more rapid in such pipes, approximating to the speed of surface flow, than in the tortuous tiny passages otherwise found in soil.

Detailed mapping of soils demonstrates that on coarse soils in

**37** An active soil-pipe (to the right of the film carton) at the junction between peat (above) and soil

**38** The pattern of percolines in the
drainage basin of Bentley Brook, near
Matlock, Derbyshire

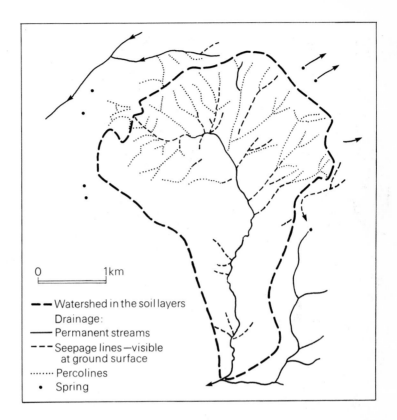

particular concentrations of water seepage take place. Seepage
routes, termed **percolines**, of deeper soil with coarser soil particles
and higher moisture contents are shown for one basin in figure 38.
These percolines converge downslope upon more prominent 'seepage
lines' where moisture flow is indicated at the surface by vegetation
and slight depressions. These in turn converge upon stream channels.
Rates of flow of moisture within the percolines in this basin were
more than 23 cm/hr in the A-horizons but showed a sharp decrease
in B-horizons to between 1 and 2 cm/hr.

The patterns of soil throughflow are evidently complex and more
work needs to be done before they can be fully understood. Nevertheless, it is clear that for most temperate areas throughflow is an
important contributor to river flow. If more were understood of the
former it might be possible to predict more accurately variations in
the latter.

*Groundwater flow and storage*
On permeable rocks, as has been pointed out, throughflow may be
supplemented, or even replaced, by groundwater flow. The long
periods of steady or very slowly declining river flow shown in figure
28 during June, are times when water is only slowly being added to
the river network. It is clear from these hydrographs that baseflow
does vary in amount but not as rapidly as throughflow.

Figure 31 summarises the processes which operate between rain
water reaching the ground and its eventual arrival in the stream
channel. The importance of infiltration capacity and bedrock per-

meability, in regulating flow into any of three routes — overland, through the soil, or into the bedrock — has been examined and the importance of throughflow stressed. The hydrographs in figures 28 and 30 show clearly the effects of overland and throughflow in producing sudden increases of streamflow. The study of these processes is important not only for increasing our understanding of soil water drainage but also in the attempts to develop flood warning systems. The importance of baseflow for maintaining river levels during dry spells is also very clear.

## Selected references

Chorley, R.J. (ed.). 1969. *Water, Earth and Man.* London: Methuen.
Weyman, D. 1975. *Runoff Processes and Streamflow Modelling.* Oxford: OUP.
Weyman, D. et al. 1975. Hydrology for schools. *Teaching Geography Occasional Paper*, no. 25. Geographical Association.

# 5

# Drainage basin morphometry

So far we have looked at the effects of precipitation, evapotranspiration and soil moisture upon the amount and rate at which water may reach a stream channel. Once in a channel it flows more rapidly through the channel network towards a point where it may be gauged. This chapter looks at the ways in which the configuration of the channel network might affect flow at the gauging station. The drainage basin is probably the most convenient unit for the study of both geomorphology and hydrology. It can be argued that much of the landscape owes its actual surface form, or **morphology**, to water action. The water can move slowly through soil and bedrock or flow in well defined channels. The pattern of the channels and their degree of incision give an area of landscape its particular morphological form. If these features can be measured using some form of analysis it is possible to describe accurately the morphology of a region.

The first worker to draw attention to the value of **morphometric analysis**, the mathematical description of the form of the landscape, was an American engineer, Robert E. Horton. In 1945 Horton investigated the relationship between morphometry, hydrology and landscape evolution. This form of analysis is now often referred to as **Horton morphometry**.

Since that date much work has been undertaken in this field and this account will be restricted to a consideration of the basic 'Laws of drainage composition' as outlined by Horton and to aspects of morphometry which are of particular importance to hydrology.

## The choice of the drainage network

There is little doubt that the principles of morphometric analysis are of value to geomorphology and hydrology but the major practical difficulty is to obtain the data with which to begin the analysis. It is necessary to define the **drainage basin** and to recognise the **drainage pattern** within that basin. It is a relatively simple matter to define the margins of the drainage basin from contoured maps by tracing the watersheds which enclose its tributaries and slopes, but we are then faced with the problem of what constitutes the 'drainage pattern'.

There are two distinct possibilities: we can either consider the **active channel network** in which water flows at the present or we can use the **valley network**. The valley network includes not only the present active channel network but also the valleys in the basin that no longer carry active flow. For example, the dry valleys of the Chalk of southern England represent a well marked valley network with only a very restricted active channel network. There is also a third category of stream channels that are normally dry but carry

**39** Byrecleuch Burn (to the west) and Tarras Water (NY415907), tributaries to Eskdale, north of Carlisle, Cumbria. The detail shows many more tributaries than appear on the Ordnance Survey maps. Peat-covered felltops with indeterminate drainage make placing of watersheds difficult. These small streams meander tightly, widening their valley floors in the process

**40** Stream networks as depicted on various Ordnance Survey maps (all reduced to same scale). The area is that covered by 1:25 000 map SS 31 NW

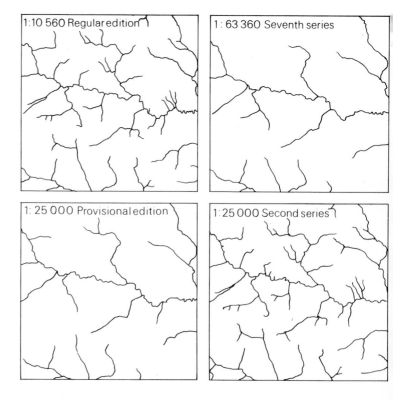

1:10 560 Regular edition

1: 63 360 Seventh series

1: 25 000 Provisional edition

1:25 000 Second series

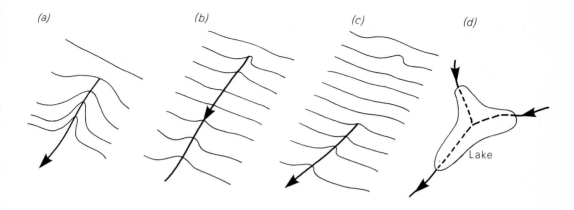

**41** Contour patterns and the insertion of valley network channels (contour interval in all cases is 25 ft [7·6 m])

*(a)*  *(b)*  *(c)*  *(d)*

Lake

water after heavy rainfall. The channel or valley network can be identified from maps, from air photographs or from field observation. The majority of morphometric studies, however, are made from maps and in that case the active channel network is the river and stream pattern as portrayed on the map. This is often a matter of using the **blue line network** shown on the map. The valley network is obtained from the pattern shown by the contours. It is clear that the pattern of both the blue lines and the contours will vary according to the scale of the map used and according to the amount of detail shown by the map maker for any given series of maps. Figure 40 shows the blue line pattern for a small area in west Devon taken from several different Ordnance Survey maps published at various scales. For ease of comparison these have all been reduced to the same scale.

If morphometric analysis is to have meaning it is necessary to compare 'like with like'. If we are comparing the morphometry of one region to another we must either compare active channel networks from one map to another or valley networks from one map to another. The scale and the cartographic methods employed must also be comparable. For morphometric studies based on British maps the best scale and map series to use is the 1:25 000 edition.

The decision as to whether to use the blue line network or the valley network depends on the purpose of the study. If the major concern is with the overall form of the landscape the valley network is preferable but for studies with a hydrological basis the active channel network could be used.

## Ordering the network

Regardless of scale, or type of network, the first essential for morphometric studies is to **order the network**. Various schemes have been suggested but for most purposes the method proposed by the American geologist A.N. Strahler is the simplest and most effective.

The procedure is straightforward if the blue line network is used but if the valley network is to be used some guide lines are needed. Valley networks are defined according to the contour pattern and the presence or absence of a blue line is immaterial. Thus in figure 41a the channel is drawn as indicated. Problems can arise with a contour pattern of the kind shown in figure 41b; A working rule, on the British 1:25 000 maps, would be to insert a valley line if at least

51

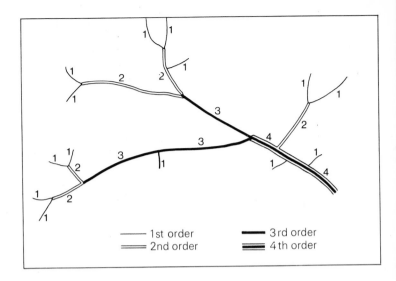

one contour in every four is 'nicked'. On other map series modification for scale and contour interval is necessary. Thus a channel would be inserted in figure 41b but not in figure 41c. Other minor problems arise such as the presence of small lakes. In this case channels are usually extended through the lake as shown in figure 41d. Man-made interference is sometimes confusing but if it is remembered that the aim is to mark the pattern of natural streams and valleys the ordering of the network should not present any real difficulty.

In the Strahler scheme for ordering the network all the 'finger tip' tributaries are designated as **first order streams.** When two first order streams join they form a **second order stream.** When two second order streams join they form a third order and so on with streams of higher orders. However, if a second order stream is joined by a first order stream it remains second order, and similarly if a third order stream is joined by a first or second order stream, and so on. The ordering system is illustrated in figure 42, which shows a fourth order basin. The fourth order basin is complete when the major stream joins another fourth, or higher, order stream. It is often helpful to trace out the drainage basin under study and to show the streams of different order in different colours.

## Horton's laws of drainage composition (or morphometry)

Once the network pattern has been ordered it is possible to investigate the relationships of stream order to other measurements that can be made within the drainage basin.

The four Horton relationships that we will illustrate are as follows:

(1) the relationship between the number of streams of each order in the drainage basin;

(2) the average length of the streams of each order;

(3) the slope, or gradient, of the streams of each order;

(4) the drainage basin area for streams of each order.

For convenience these relationships will all be illustrated from data taken from the Ordnance Survey 1:25 000 maps (provisional edition). In all cases the data are for fourth order basins located on individual rock types and are for the valley network. All the values in this chapter are in Imperial units as these are considered to be most suitable for comparison to work undertaken by students from the most readily available Ordnance Survey maps.

*Stream number*
If we take a fourth order catchment located wholly on granite bedrock on Dartmoor and count from the map the number of streams of each order (table 14), we can plot the result on semi-logarithmic paper (see appendix) as shown in figure 43. The four points fall more or less on a straight line, suggesting something very close to a geometric relationship between the number of streams and their order. We can use the graph to read off the number of streams there should be of each order if there were a true geometric relationship. The graph shows that for every fourth order stream there should be three third order streams, eleven second order streams and about thirty-six first order streams. This compares with an observed three third order, nine second order and forty first order. It is a valuable property of semi-logarithmic graphs that geometric relationships are always indicated by straight lines.

Figure 44 and table 15 show data averaged over twelve fourth order Dartmoor granite basins. The similarity between these results and those for the single basin is remarkable and whenever such studies have been made they confirm that there is always an approximate geometric relationship between stream order and stream number. This is, in fact, the first Horton law of morphometry: stream number is related to stream order by a geometric relationship.

*Stream length*
To find the average length of the streams corresponding to each order the total length of all the first, second, third and fourth order streams needs to be measured. This is time consuming but can be undertaken either by the use of a map wheel or by carefully measuring along each stream length on the map with a length of thread. The total length of each stream order is divided by the number of streams of that order to give the average length.

The stream lengths for the single Dartmoor catchment, given in table 14, are plotted in figure 45. The corresponding plot for the twelve basins in table 15 is given in figure 46. The straight line graphs obtained illustrate Horton's second law of morphometry — the average lengths of streams of each of the different orders in a drainage basin form a geometric series.

*Stream slope (or gradient)*
To obtain values for the gradient of the streams of differing order it is necessary to measure the total fall in height of the streams of each order. Thus the fall in height of each and every first order stream is found by considering the contour pattern of the map. The total fall of all the first order streams is divided by their total length (obtained above) to give a value for their average gradient. This is normally

53

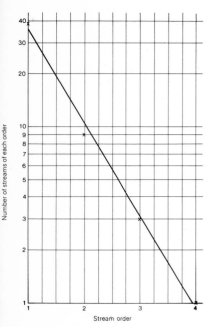

**43** Relationship of stream number to stream order for the individual fourth order basin from table 14

**Table 14**   *Morphometric data for a single fourth order basin on the Dartmoor granite*

| Order | Number | Length in miles | Gradient in ft/mile | Area in square miles |
|---|---|---|---|---|
| 1 | 39 | 0.35 | 374 | 0.156 |
| 2 | 9 | 0.575 | 283 | 0.602 |
| 3 | 3 | 2.10 | 155 | 3.314 |
| 4 | 1 | 3.41 | 105 | 12.602 |

**Table 15**   *Morphometric data averaged from twelve fourth-order basins on the Dartmoor granite*

| Order | Number | Length in miles | Gradient in ft/mile | Area in square miles | Total length of stream in miles |
|---|---|---|---|---|---|
| 1 | 44.9 | 0.43 | 302 | 0.14 | 19.35 |
| 2 | 10.6 | 0.76 | 245 | 0.61 | 8.06 |
| 3 | 2.8 | 1.90 | 161 | 2.58 | 5.32 |
| 4 | 1 | 3.71 | 125 | 10.38 | 3.71 |

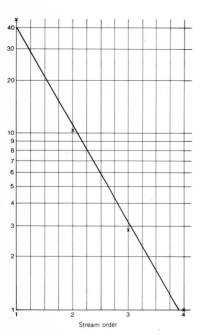

**44** Relationship of stream number to stream order, average for the twelve basins from table 15

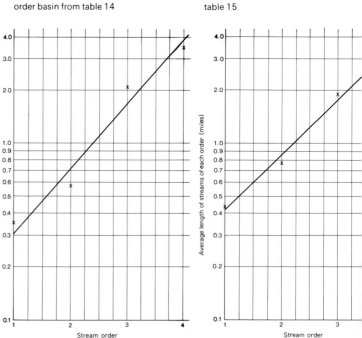

**45** Relationship of average stream length to stream order for the individual fourth order basin from table 14

**46** Relationship of average stream length to stream order for the twelve basins from table 15

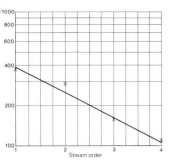

**7** Relationship of average slope to stream order for the individual fourth order basin from table 14

Stream order

**8** Relationship of drainage basin area to stream order for the individual fourth order basin from table 14

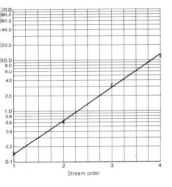

Stream order

**9** Relationship of stream number to stream order for the channel network of the USA from table 16

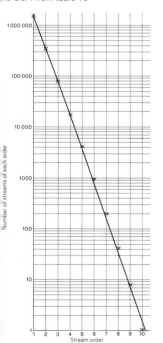

Number of streams of each order

Stream order

expressed in feet per mile. The procedure is repeated for the second, third and fourth order streams.

A semi-logarithmic graph of the data for stream order and gradient from table 14 is given in figure 47. Once more a straight line geometric relationship is strongly suggested; low order streams have steep gradients, higher order streams have low gradients. This is the third Horton law.

*Drainage basin area*
To investigate the relationship of drainage basin area to stream order it is first necessary to divide the fourth order basin into sub-catchments corresponding to each of the streams recognised in the original drainage net. This sub-division is made from a careful con-sideration of the contour pattern.

The easiest way to measure the area of each individual basin is to trace the pattern of catchments onto tracing paper and then to super-impose the tracing paper onto squared graph paper. Then by count-ing squares it is possible to obtain values for each catchment and to work out the average basin area for streams of each order.

The computations for the single fourth order Dartmoor basin in table 14 are graphed in figure 48. Once more a straight line and therefore geometric relationship is suggested and plotting the data from table 15 would confirm this relationship. So once again we see a clear link between stream order and area of drainage basins. This is Horton's fourth law.

## Extension of Horton's laws

A plot of the number of streams against order is given in figure 49 (data in table 16) which shows that for the whole stream network of the USA there is a regularity in the relationship as close as in the smaller drainage systems on Dartmoor. In the USA example the tenth order network corresponds to the drainage basin area of the River Mississippi and is developed on a wide range of different rock types. If the data of table 16 on average stream length and average drainage basin area are similarly graphed they would show an equal regularity. The discovery of these four basic relationships or regu-

Table 16    *Morphometric data for the active channel network of the United States of America*

| Order | Number | Average length in miles | Total length in miles | Average catchment area in square miles |
|---|---|---|---|---|
| 1 | 1 570 000 | 1.0 | 1 570 000 | 1.0 |
| 2 | 350 000 | 2.3 | 810 000 | 4.7 |
| 3 | 80 000 | 5.3 | 420 000 | 23.0 |
| 4 | 18 000 | 12.0 | 220 000 | 109.0 |
| 5 | 4 200 | 28.0 | 116 000 | 518.0 |
| 6 | 950 | 64.0 | 61 000 | 2 460.0 |
| 7 | 200 | 147.0 | 30 000 | 11 700.0 |
| 8 | 41 | 338.0 | 14 000 | 55 600.0 |
| 9 | 8 | 777.0 | 6 200 | 264 000.0 |
| 10 | 1 | 1 800.0 | 1 800 | 1 250 000.0 |

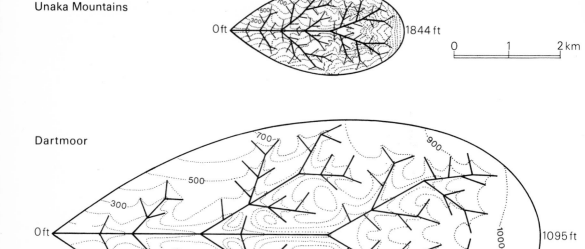

Unaka Mountains

0 ft — 1844 ft

0    1    2 km

Dartmoor

0 ft — 1095 ft

larities in drainage networks was of very great significance because for the first time it enabled landscape to be 'measured' in a more precise way.

## Morphometry and lithology

The four measures of morphometry made for the twelve Dartmoor granite basins go a long way towards fully describing the shape and form of the Dartmoor scenery. It is possible to draw up a model Dartmoor granite basin using the average values from table 15. Figure 50 illustrates idealised (or 'model') fourth order catchments for two quite different granite areas. One of these basins is constructed from data for the Unaka Mountains in the Appalachians, USA and the other is for Dartmoor.

The 'model' for each area is based only upon the 'average' data for each area. It is quite obvious that the typical Dartmoor granite fourth order basin is very different from the typical Unaka Mountain basin. The Dartmoor basin is much larger, has gentler, more rounded slopes, with a flattish watershed and a relatively open network of streams. The Unaka catchment has a relative relief of 1644 ft (compared with 1095 ft for Dartmoor), much steeper slopes, and a higher channel density. These two 'models' therefore summarise in a precise way the characteristics and differences of two quite separate granite areas.

If the same form of stream ordering and measurement is undertaken for basins situated on differing **lithologies** (rock types) we can investigate whether Horton's laws still apply and whether the morphometry differs from one lithology to another. All the data presented are from the same series of 1:25 000 maps.

Table 17    *Morphometric data averaged from eight fourth order basins on the Tertiary sands and gravels of Hampshire*

| Order | Number | Length in miles | Gradient in ft/mile | Area in square miles | Total length of streams in miles |
|---|---|---|---|---|---|
| 1 | 108 | 0.214 | 229 | 0.061 | 23.11 |
| 2 | 25 | 0.42 | 104 | 0.22 | 10.50 |
| 3 | 5 | 1.22 | 56 | 1.10 | 6.10 |
| 4 | 1 | 4.11 | 26 | 8.90 | 4.11 |

Table 18    *Morphometric data averaged from ten fourth order basins on the Chalk of Salisbury Plain*

| Order | Number | Length in miles | Gradient in ft/mile | Area in square miles | Total length of streams in miles |
|---|---|---|---|---|---|
| 1 | 25 | 0.322 | 255 | 0.106 | 8.05 |
| 2 | 8 | 0.527 | 131 | 0.385 | 4.21 |
| 3 | 3 | 0.864 | 67 | 1.42 | 2.59 |
| 4 | 1 | 1.42 | 35 | 5.18 | 1.42 |

Table 17 gives the data averaged from eight fourth order basins situated on the Tertiary sands and gravels of the New Forest of Hampshire. Table 18 gives similar data for ten fourth order basins on the Chalk of Salisbury Plain. The Chalk networks are composed almost entirely of dry valleys. The information from tables 17 and 18 can be plotted on graphs similar to those in figures 44 to 47.

It will be found that the Horton laws still apply in that the semi-logarithmic plots approximate to straight lines, but the slope of the lines is clearly different for the three lithologies. It is an interesting exercise to try and draw out the model drainage basins for these three lithologies to correspond with those illustrated in figure 50.

From this exercise it can be seen that different lithologies give rise to different morphometry within the climate of southern England, although the morphometry may be related to climates in the past. It would be of great value to geomorphology to see whether the same lithology (for example granite) gives a different morphometry when the landscape is developed under a different climate, for example, fourth order granite basin morphometry developed in a humid tropical or semi-arid region. This valuable comparison is difficult as maps at corresponding scales and with similar drainage and contour detail are difficult to obtain for such widely scattered localities.

## Morphometry and hydrology

So far we have considered morphometry in terms of describing the landscape. It also has a valuable part to play in the study of hydrology.

*Drainage density*

In addition to the four Horton laws described above, many additional measures of the morphometry of drainage basins and networks have been proposed in the literature. The most useful single measure is undoubtedly that of **drainage density**. Drainage density is calculated

57

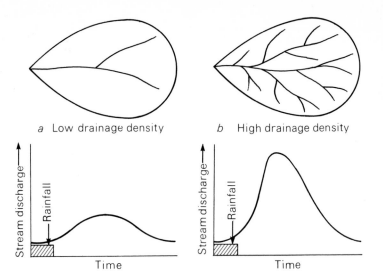

51 Relationship of drainage density to stream hydrograph

*a*  Low drainage density          *b*  High drainage density

by dividing the total area of the basin by the total length of either the active channel or the valley network. Thus an individual basin can have two drainage densities.

The data for the blue line network of the tenth order basin given in table 16 give the following drainage density:

$$\frac{\text{Total channel length in miles}}{\text{Total area in square miles}} = \frac{3\,249\,000}{1\,250\,000} = 2.59 \text{ miles of channel per square mile}$$

For the average Dartmoor valley network (see table 15) the drainage density is:

$$\frac{36.44 \text{ miles}}{10.38 \text{ square miles}} = 3.51 \text{ miles/square mile}$$

The drainage densities for the valley networks for 'average' fourth order basins of the New Forest and Salisbury Plain can be calculated from tables 17 and 18; the total length of streams of each order is given in the tables.

The drainage density is of importance in hydrology as it is one of the factors that control the speed of run-off following a period of precipitation. Water moves relatively slowly through a soil cover (see chapter 4) compared to the velocity it achieves once it has reached an active stream channel. The greater the drainage density the faster the run-off; therefore with a high drainage density the stream hydrograph for run-off responds more rapidly to precipitation and the hydrograph is more peaked. Thus flooding for a given quantity of rainfall is more likely in a region with a high drainage density. This effect is illustrated in figure 51.

The drainage density found in an area is related to a number of factors. We have already seen that the underlying lithology is one of the controls, and another is the magnitude of the mean annual flood. The relationship of the size of the mean annual flood to the drainage density for Wales, Wisconsin and the north-east USA is shown in figure 52. It can be seen that basins in each of the three areas shown have a different magnitude of relationship between mean annual flood and drainage density, but the parallel trends demonstrate similar rates of increase in drainage density with an increasing size

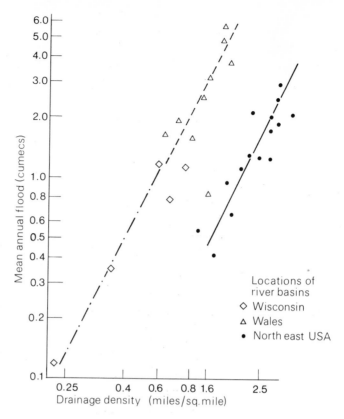

**52** Relationship of mean annual flood to drainage density in Wales, Wisconsin, and north-east USA

Mean annual flood (cumecs)

Drainage density (miles/sq.mile)

Locations of river basins
◇ Wisconsin
△ Wales
• North east USA

of mean annual flood. Another major factor is thought to be rainfall intensity: the higher the rainfall intensity the greater the drainage density. This may explain why many of the highest drainage densities are from semi-arid regions or from areas of badland topography. Drainage densities for valley networks in excess of 200 miles per square mile have been recorded from the badlands of South Dakota. Factors such as soil type (related to lithology), slope, vegetation and land use will also have some effect in controlling drainage density.

In times of abnormal flood the length of the active channel network will extend far beyond that shown by the blue lines on the map. For a single catchment on the Mendip Hills, Somerset, for the abnormal flood of July 1968, it has been calculated that the stream length (and therefore the drainage density) increased by a factor of ten over the 'normal' blue line network given on the relevant maps.

It is likely that the differences between the blue line network and the valley network for a given area is a measure of changes in climate over a long period of time. Exactly what elements of the climate have changed is not so easy to judge!

An instructive field exercise is to map the drainage network for a small area after a flood and to compare this to the blue line network on the map. The flood network can be observed quite easily after the flood has passed, the temporary stream channels either causing minor gullying or affecting grass and other vegetation.

A useful map exercise is to obtain figures for the length of active channel networks as shown by blue lines. Convert these figures to drainage densities and then compare the densities between differing areas of lithology and/or in relationship to mean annual rainfall. For this exercise it is not necessary to order the network, although comparisons should be made on maps of comparable scales.

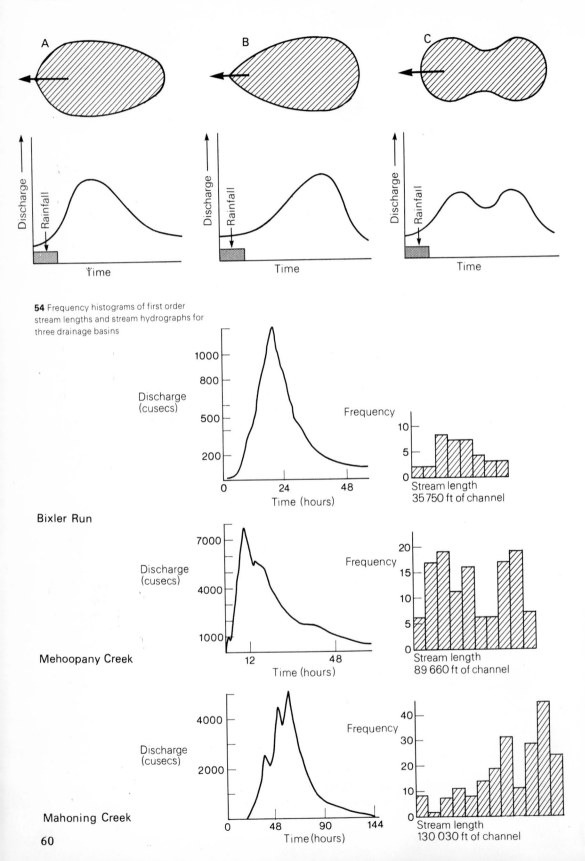

**53** Basin shape and the stream hydrograph

A

B

C

Discharge
Rainfall
Time

Discharge
Rainfall
Time

Discharge
Rainfall
Time

**54** Frequency histograms of first order stream lengths and stream hydrographs for three drainage basins

**Bixler Run**

Discharge (cusecs)
1000
800
500
200
0
24
48
Time (hours)

Frequency
10
5
0
Stream length
35 750 ft of channel

**Mehoopany Creek**

Discharge (cusecs)
7000
4000
1000
12
48
Time (hours)

Frequency
20
15
10
5
0
Stream length
89 660 ft of channel

**Mahoning Creek**

Discharge (cusecs)
4000
2000
0
48
90
144
Time (hours)

Frequency
40
30
20
10
0
Stream length
130 030 ft of channel

*Hydrology and basin shape*

Drainage density is important in affecting the form of the stream hydrograph but basin shape and the distribution of the channel lines within the basin can also modify its shape.

In general terms the effects of basin shape are illustrated in figure 53. In example A the peak of the hydrograph occurs relatively quickly after the storm rainfall. In example B, which approximates to the most commonly occurring basin shape, the peak of the hydrograph occurs with a longer delay after the storm peak. In those cases where the basin has a composite shape the hydrograph form will be more complex. Example C shows the form for an 'hour glass' shaped basin.

For all the examples in figure 53 it is assumed that the storm rainfall occurs at the same time over the whole basin and with the same intensity, and that run-off characteristics (such as infiltration) are similar in all cases.

It is difficult to find actual examples that illustrate these relationships, perhaps because of the nature of the assumptions! However, a similar form of analysis which has produced interesting results compares the shape of the stream hydrograph to stream lengths. The length of each and every first order stream is measured from its beginning down through the whole channel length (including streams of higher orders) to the stream gauging station and these are tabulated. The lengths are then arranged as a histogram. Three examples are given in figure 54, based on the work of hydrologist William F. Rogers undertaken in the American mid-west. The similarity in form of the stream hydrographs and the frequency diagrams of stream lengths is striking and shows that the two are related.

The morphometry of drainage basins results from a complex of factors. Climate, lithology and the time for which the climate has been operative are the three major elements. This corresponds closely to the statement outlined by W.M. Davis some eighty years ago about the importance of process, structure and stage in the development of landforms, which forms the basis of most geomorphological teaching today. The methods of morphometric analysis outlined in this chapter takes Davis' views a little further in that they give us a technique with which to describe the landscape so that more detailed comparisons can be made between areas. Stream order numbering also provides a useful framework for planning field work sampling when measuring changes which take place in a downstream direction. Samples, measurements of discharge, meander size, bed load size, and so on, can be taken from first order streams and compared with second and third order and so on.

Morphometry is, however, essentially a descriptive technique and does not supply the answers to *how* the processes actually form the present day landscape. We can show, for example, that landscapes developed on differing rock types are indeed different but not why they are different. The climate may vary from area to area but we do not fully understand which climatic variables are responsible for the differences in landscape; it could be rainfall intensity, mean annual rainfall or a range of other individual climatic factors. We do not yet know how lithology affects landscape evolution — is it due to soil and vegetation differences or is it due to the rate of weathering and

If you can obtain stream hydrographs for storms it would be an interesting project to compare the form of these to the frequency of stream length for the basin concerned. It is best to undertake this work for medium-sized basins (in the range between ten and a hundred square miles), which as far as possible have similar soil and vegetation cover. The channel length in figure 54 was for the blue line network. In Britain it is best to use the 1:25 000 maps.

erosion of differing rock types? Finally we are always faced with the difficulty that the contemporary landscape might in fact have evolved when the climatic regime was very different to that of the present day.

Morphometric analysis was first developed by Horton in relation to problems of soil erosion but its applied significance continues because of its application to problems of flood run-off. The technique was extensively used by the Institute of Hydrology in Britain for investigating flood peaks and their relationships with the morphometric characteristics of basins in an attempt to find what factors contribute to flooding.

## Selected references

Brunsden, D. 1968. *Dartmoor*. Geographical Association.
Horton, R.E. 1945. Erosional development of streams and their drainage basins: a hydrophysical approach to quantitative geomorphology. *Bull. Geol. Soc. America.* **56**, 275–370.
Institute of Hydrology. 1975. *Flood Studies Report*, vol. 1. Natural Environment Research Council.

# 6

# River velocity – its variation and controls

River discharge was considered in chapter 2 together with methods for its measurement. At any point along a river discharge depends upon the amount of water being delivered and the velocity at which it can move past that point. The former depends as we have seen upon precipitation, throughflow and the channel network. We shall now turn our attention to river velocity.

## Channel gradient

The steeper the angle of any channel the faster the water flows down it, since gravity has a more direct effect. In river channels this is true, other things being equal. However the angle of slope of the channel is usually so small that it is measured more easily as a gradient than in degrees. A gradient of 1 in 100 means that the channel drops 1 m vertically for every 100 m it travels horizontally. Measurement of gradient in the field is often made difficult by bushes and other obstacles obscuring the line of sight. It is usually most easily and accurately done by looking along a level sighting line to a pole held vertically upon the water surface at one point and marking the place on the pole where the level sighting line intersects it. The pole is then moved as far along the stream as possible and a new mark placed where the same sighting line intersects it. The distance between these two marks and the distance along the stream course between the two points (expressed in the same units) gives a fairly accurate measurement of the gradient of the stream.

A simple experiment using running water, ice cubes (preferably dyed) and a length of guttering can be set up to demonstrate this relationship. Connect a hose-pipe to a tap and maintain constant flow whilst varying the gradient of the gutter and timing the passage of ice cubes over a measured length.

Research workers have found that velocity (V) actually varies in proportion to the square root of the gradient (s), i.e. $V \propto \sqrt{s}$ (or $s^{0.5}$).

## Velocity changes downstream

As the gradient increases, then, other things being equal, the velocity also increases at a rate proportional to the square root of the gradient. Figure 55 shows changes in gradient as one moves down-stream along the River Clarach in Dyfed, Wales. This is termed the **long profile** of the river and can easily be drawn from the map by following the river course with the edge of a sheet of paper, marking it whenever a contour is crossed. The actual measured gradient of

**55** Gradient and velocity along R. Clarach, Dyfed, Wales

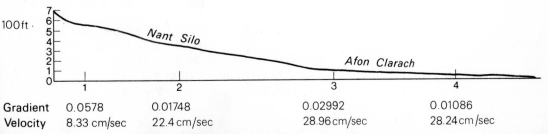

| | | | | |
|---|---|---|---|---|
| Gradient | 0.0578 | 0.01748 | 0.02992 | 0.01086 |
| Velocity | 8.33 cm/sec | 22.4 cm/sec | 28.96 cm/sec | 28.24 cm/sec |

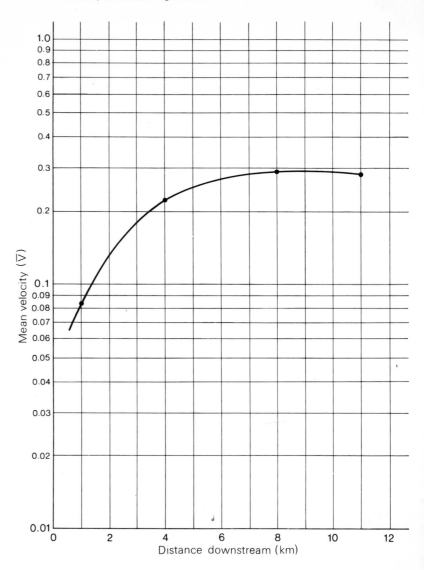

**56** Graph showing mean velocity of R. Clarach, Dyfed, Wales, along its course

the channel and the velocity of the water in that section are given at various points along the profile of the river in figure 55. However, whereas gradient decreases downstream the velocity does not. This is clearly shown in the graph of the results in figure 56. Indeed the graph shows quite a considerable increase in velocity downstream for most of the river profile, except for the final section as the tidal part of the channel is approached. This overall increase in velocity downstream is not unusual; measurements of rivers in humid climates show that in general velocity is either fairly constant or increases downstream, despite the fact that the gradient decreases. Since we can see that along the profile of a river velocity does not decrease with gradient downstream, it is evident that 'other things' are not 'equal' along the river profile. A number of 'other things' affect the velocity of flow of water in a river channel besides gradient.

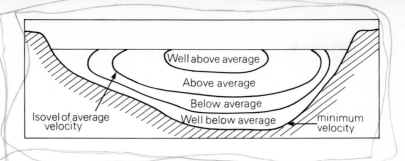

Table 19    *Values of n in Manning's formula for natural streams*

| Stream description | Channel state | | | |
| | bad | fair | good | best |
| --- | --- | --- | --- | --- |
| *Minor streams (< 30 m wide at bank-full)* | | | | |
| Lowland | | | | |
|    Clean, straight, no rifts or deep pools | 0.033 | 0.030 | 0.0275 | 0.025 |
|    Some weeds or stones | 0.040 | 0.035 | 0.033 | 0.030 |
|    Clean, winding, some pools or shoals | 0.045 | 0.040 | 0.035 | 0.033 |
|    More stones | 0.060 | 0.055 | 0.050 | 0.045 |
|    Sluggish reaches, weedy, deep pools | 0.080 | 0.070 | 0.060 | 0.050 |
|    Very weedy reaches | 0.150 | 0.125 | 0.100 | 0.075 |
| Upland (no vegetation in channel except at bank-full; banks steep) | | | | |
|    Gravel, cobbles and some boulders on bed | 0.050 | 0.040 | 0.035 | 0.030 |
|    Cobbles and large boulders on bed | 0.070 | 0.060 | 0.050 | 0.040 |
| *Major streams (> 30 m wide at bank-full)* | | | | |
|    Regular reach with no boulders or weed | 0.060 | 0.050 | 0.035 | 0.025 |
|    Irregular and rough section | 0.100 | 0.080 | 0.050 | 0.035 |

## Channel roughness

The water as it flows is in contact with the channel bed and banks. As we saw in chapter 2 the velocity of water flowing in a river channel decreases rapidly towards the banks and bed, and this is due to the frictional drag. Examples are given in figures 4 and 5 and are generalised in figure 57.

The amount of friction exerted against the flow of the water depends upon the roughness of the bed and banks. Thus friction in a small stream in a mountainous region, with boulders breaking through the water surface, will be quite high compared with the friction in a smooth, fine clay-lined channel farther downstream. The large amount of friction in a mountain stream is shown by the turbulence of the water compared with the much smoother flow downstream in less rough channels. The impression that the river is flowing more slowly in these lower, less turbulent, sections, would be disproved by measurement of the velocity.

Velocity, then, is inversely related to channel roughness. This can be expressed symbolically as $V \propto 1/n$, where n is a measure of the roughness of a stream channel and is known as **Manning's n**. Typical values of n are given in table 19. It can be seen that n varies not only

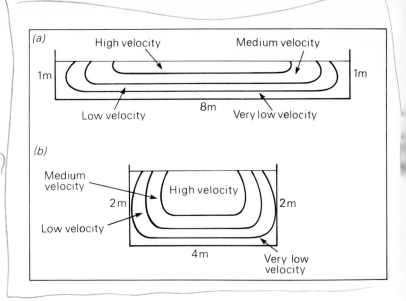

(a)

High velocity    Medium velocity

1m    1m

8m

Low velocity    Very low velocity

(b)

Medium velocity    High velocity

2m    2m

Low velocity

4m

Very low velocity

with the channel materials but also with channel sinuosity, shape, size and the extent to which it is choked with weeds. The last factor, weeds, may often be underrated but is a major influence in small streams. It clearly varies seasonally, so that Manning's n can vary seasonally for any particular channel reach as well as with the stage (level) of river flow. Table 19 may be used to give an estimate of Manning's n for any reach of any stream at any stage.

## Channel shape

The shape of a channel also significantly affects friction between the channel sides and floor and the water. Figure 58 shows the effect of friction in a broad, shallow channel compared with a deeper, narrower one. In figure 58a the effect of friction is felt very strongly over almost the whole of the cross-sectional area of the channel. Figure 58b shows that average velocity for the whole of the channel cross-section will be much higher.

In both channels the cross-sectional area (A) is the same: in 58a $A = 8 \times 1\ m^2$, and in 58b $A = 4 \times 2\ m^2$; but the length of the bed and banks across the section in contact with the water, i.e. the **wetted perimeter**, is not the same: in 58a it is $1 + 8 + 1 = 10$ m, and in 58b it is $2 + 4 + 2 = 8$ m.

We can compare the efficiency of the shape of one channel with that of another by comparing the ratios of the cross-sectional area and the wetted perimeter of each. These ratios, known as the **hydraulic radius (R)** of the channels are, for 58a $8/10 = 0.8$, and for 58b $8/8 = 1.0$. Thus the higher the value of R, the more efficient the channel shape.

In table 20 the values of R have been calculated for two locations along the small stream in Anglesey, Wales, from which figures 4 and 5 were compiled. It is clear that in the deeper, narrower channel, only a short distance downstream from the other channel reach, the hydraulic radius increases. Therefore if you have completed the isovels suggested for figure 5 they should indicate faster channel flow in this more efficient section (i.e. assuming similar channel materials and negligible effect of gradient).

Table 20    *Measurements made at profiles 1 and 2*
*(figures 4 and 5) on a small stream in Anglesey, Wales*

|  | Profile 1 | Profile 2 |
|---|---|---|
| Gradient | s = 1/780 | s = 1/200 |
| Area | A = 1.0528 m² | A = 0.6935 m² |
| Hydraulic radius | R = 0.2149 m | R = 0.1926 m |
| Wetted perimeter | WP = 4.90 m | WP = 3.60 m |
| Manning's n | n = 0.043 | n = 0.055 |

## Channel size

In calculating the value of R for a river only the cross-sectional area of the channel actually occupied by water is measured, i.e. the wetted part. Therefore the R value applies to a particular point along the river channel with a particular depth of water. The value varies as the depth of water changes, the channel becoming more efficient as water depth increases so that the water will flow faster. The most efficient depth therefore is when the river is level with the banks. This condition is called **bank-full**, and bank-full discharge is commonly used when investigating possible relationships between discharge and, for example, channel width or channel pattern (see chapter 9).

Similarly when two tributaries meet, the channel below their confluence will be more efficient than the two separate tributary channels, owing to its smaller wetted perimeter. Consequently its shape or gradient may change to compensate for the increased energy available.

The velocity of water in a river channel, then, depends both on the efficiency of the channel shape and its size as expressed by its hydraulic radius (R) and on gradient and roughness. As the value of R increases, the channel shape and size is more efficient and so the velocity also increases. In practice this relationship, like that between velocity and gradient, has been found not to be direct. In this case the cubed power of the velocity is proportional to the square of the hydraulic radius. Thus $V \propto R^{2/3}$ (the cube root of $R^2$).

Putting the three relationships together we can see that the velocity of a river in its channel varies with the gradient (s), the roughness (1/n), and the hydraulic radius (R), or:

$$V \propto (s)^{1/2} \times (1/n) \times (R)^{2/3}$$

By measuring these values at points along a large number of rivers of all different sizes it has been found that:

$$\text{Velocity} = \frac{s^{1/2} \cdot R^{2/3}}{n} \text{ in m}^3/\text{sec}$$

where n (the Manning coefficient) varies between 0.01 for very smooth channels and 0.07 for very rough, weed-choked channels (table 19), s is the gradient, and R is the hydraulic radius measured in metric units.

We can now see that the texture of the channel and its shape and size (expressed as its hydraulic radius) can offset the decrease in gradient by reducing the overall friction on the water and can thereby allow the river to maintain its velocity along the whole of its length.

Manning's formula: $V = \dfrac{s^{\frac{1}{2}} \cdot R^{\frac{2}{3}}}{n}$

| | No. | Log. |
|---|---|---|
| s | | |
| $s^{\frac{1}{2}} = \div 2$ | | |
| R | | |
| $\times 2$ | | |
| $R^{\frac{2}{3}} = \div 3$ | | |
| $s^{\frac{1}{2}}$ | | |
| $R^{\frac{2}{3}}$ | | |
| Add | | |
| n | | |
| Subtract | | |

Using our final equation, that $V = s^{1/2} \cdot R^{2/3}/n$ m³/sec, we can now obtain a rough approximation of the mean velocity over the channel, provided we know the values of n, s and R. Slope can easily be measured in metres drop per 100 m along the water surface: the hydraulic radius can be obtained by sounding the depth of the channel and drawing its cross-profile, from which the necessary values of A and the wetted perimeter can be measured. Finally the value of n can be estimated with a fair degree of accuracy using table 19, although differences in the size of rivers may make this estimation confusing. It is a method used by US water engineers in channels for which no data exist, but they use more detailed charts for calculating Manning's n.

The values of n and s given in table 20 were obtained for those channels given in the two profiles (figures 4 and 5) in chapter 2. Using these values, and the calculations of R made earlier in this chapter, the mean velocity can be calculated and compared with the mean velocity obtained by the detailed measurements used to draw an isovel diagram in chapter 2. The layout for calculating this using logarithm tables is given in figure 59.

We have seen an advantage in making field measurements of velocity rather than relying upon observational assumptions since the eye can deceptively confuse rate of flow with degrees of turbulence. Measurements lead to a questioning of such assumptions and thereby to greater understanding of the factors influencing river flow velocity. We have seen that these factors include the channel gradient and its shape, and the bed and bank materials. In most rivers bed materials are at times moved (e.g. in flood), so the shape of the channel can be altered by scouring. This produces a deeper, more efficient channel and, thereby, more energy for further scouring or for an increase in velocity. As we shall see further in chapter 8 the size and amount of material moved depends upon the velocity, so the inter-relationships are quite complex. The depth of water in a channel frequently varies from day to day, as implied by figure 28, so velocity also varies.

Variations in discharge are looked at further in chapter 7, following which we shall look at the load carried by streams.

# 7

# Floods and flow frequencies

In times when water supplies were all locally obtained, when sewage
disposal presented no problems and when land was so plentiful that
areas prone to flooding were accepted as being limited in use to
occasional pasturage, for wild fowl or for rushes for thatch, there
was little need to know the likelihood of low flows or of floods.
That they occurred could be accepted and permanently allowed for.
Such times have passed. Today there is pressure on land for building
and for increased agricultural production. There are the increasing
difficulties, very apparent in the 1976 drought even in a land so rich
in water as Britain, of obtaining adequate water supplies while retaining a river level sufficient to dilute the increasing amounts of effluent
and to maintain flows for fishing, boating and other uses. Develop-
ments involving water must now be carefully planned. To fulfil
demands, without waste and without damaging the environment,
planners and engineers must be able to calculate as accurately as
possible the probable daily flows of rivers for years ahead. It requires
careful and continuous measurement of discharge variations over as
large a number of years as possible, and constant measurement of
water quality — its temperature and its sediment and chemical
content.

In Britain records of flows of some major rivers have been kept
over quite long periods. Records have been kept for the River
Thames at Teddington, for example, since 1883. For most large
rivers records commence in the 1950s and 1960s, and do not yet
provide a very reliable set of records for predicting the likelihood
and magnitude of infrequent events such as major floods or droughts.
Since these records are all that exist, however, they are used. Techniques for making predictions are fairly simple and are of widespread
application, although reliability depends upon the accuracy and
length of the records.

## Probabilities

It would be reasonable to assume that given a fairly constant climate,
the amount of water flowing down a river's course each year would
vary evenly about an average value. Any values which vary uniformly
about an average or **mean** value in this way are said to be **normally
distributed**. That is to say, if sufficient measurements were plotted
to form a graph they would produce a bell-shaped curve, as illustrated in figure 60. Data which vary in this way can be easily
examined and used for prediction.

The total annual discharges of the River Thames at Teddington
are converted to run-off for comparison with precipitation figures
(see chapter 3). The run-off at Teddington over 90 years, grouped
into 20 mm classes, is given in the first two columns of table 21.

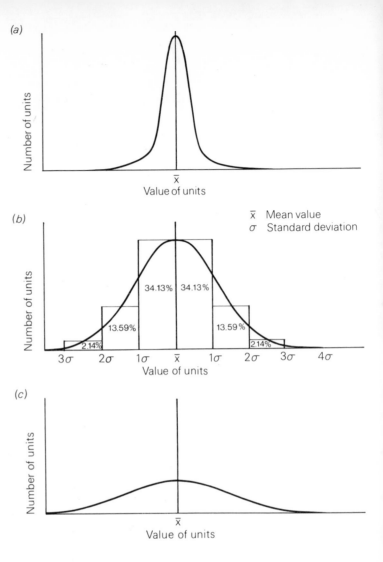

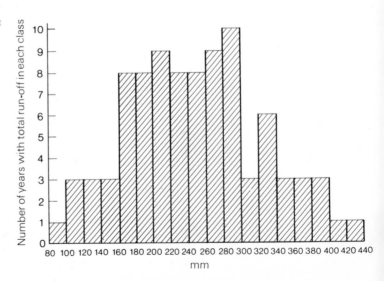

**61** Annual natural run-off for R. Thames at Teddington (1883-1972) in mm

Table 21    *Annual natural run-off for R. Thames at Teddington*
*(1883–1972) in mm*

| mm per annum | No. of years with run-off within the class value | % of total number of years | Cumulative % |
|---|---|---|---|
| 81–100 | 1 | 1.11 | 1.11 |
| 101–120 | 3 | 3.33 | 4.44 |
| 121–140 | 3 | 3.33 | 7.77 |
| 141–160 | 3 | 3.33 | 11.10 |
| 161–180 | 8 | 8.88 | 19.98 |
| 181–200 | 8 | 8.88 | 28.86 |
| 201–220 | 9 | 9.99 | 38.85 |
| 221–240 | 8 | 8.88 | 47.73 |
| 241–260 | 8 | 8.88 | 56.61 |
| 261–280 | 9 | 9.99 | 66.60 |
| 281–300 | 10 | 11.11 | 77.61 |
| 301–320 | 3 | 3.33 | 81.04 |
| 321–340 | 6 | 6.66 | 87.70 |
| 341–360 | 3 | 3.33 | 91.03 |
| 361–380 | 3 | 3.33 | 94.36 |
| 381–400 | 3 | 3.33 | 97.69 |
| 401–420 | 1 | 1.11 | 98.80 |
| 421–440 | 1 | 1.11 | 99.91 |

Total: 90 years

These values are plotted in figure 61 and form a histogram which rises to a peak and tails off fairly uniformly about a central value, similar to the bell-shaped curve and histogram in figure 59b.

From the graph in figure 61 it would be possible to say that the average annual discharge should be somewhere around 240 mm, and that discharges of less than 160 mm or more than 300 mm are very much less likely to occur than values between these two figures. It is possible to calculate how much less likely if the values are plotted differently. To do this the frequencies of flows, given in the second column of table 21, need to be expressed as percentages of the total number of years of the record (90 years). These are recorded in the third column. Next, each percentage value is added, cumulatively, to produce the last column. The figures in this column thus give as a percentage the years in which run-off did not exceed the highest value of the relevant class, e.g. in 11% of the years run-off did not exceed 160 mm; in approximately 78% of the years run-off did not exceed 300 mm.

It is thus possible to say that there is a probability that in 11 years out of 100 (i.e. 11%) run-off will not exceed 160 mm, and similarly that in 22 years out of 100 (100 − 78%) run-off will exceed 300 mm. This leaves 67 years out of 100 when run-off will be between 160 and 300 mm.

However, it is only possible to say that in 95% of the years run-off will not exceed some value between 381 mm and 400 mm, which is not accurate enough (see below). To overcome this difficulty the values given in the last column of table 21 can be plotted on a graph, as in figure 62. From this **summation curve** intermediate values can be read – the average (or mean) value is given by that corresponding

71

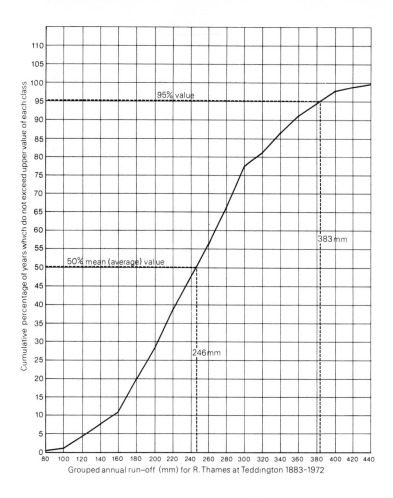

**62** Summation curve of annual natural run-off for R. Thames at Teddington (1883-1972)

*Cumulative percentage of years which do not exceed upper value of each class*

95% value

50% mean (average) value

383 mm

246 mm

Grouped annual run-off (mm) for R. Thames at Teddington 1883-1972

to 50% and is 246 mm. We can now say with some accuracy that in 95% of the years run-off will not exceed 383 mm.

The value of a graph such as figure 62 is clear, but its accuracy is somewhat impaired by the fact that it is a curve. This can be easily overcome by plotting the same values on **normal probability paper,** graph paper so designed that a summation curve of normally distributed data is drawn out into a straight line. This can be seen, with slight irregularities in the distribution, in figure 63. Values are read off as for the summation curve; the mean value is shown to be 246 mm as before, but now the 95% value is given, more precisely, as 384 mm instead of 383 mm. This may seem a very slight difference but actually represents just over 2170 million gallons of water a year in the River Thames. This is approximately the total amount of water taken from the whole of this part of the river basin each week for water supplies.

*Average annual run-off*
The irregularities in figure 63 mean that readings taken from it can only be approximations. A better approximation to the mean value from cumulative frequency graphs of this kind, instead of taking

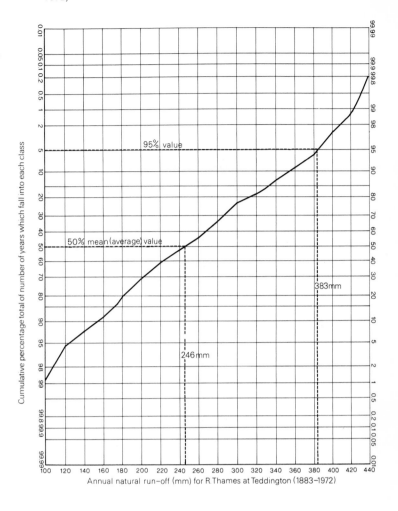

**63** Probability curve of annual natural run-off for R. Thames at Teddington (1883-1972)

Cumulative percentage total of number of years which fall into each class

Annual natural run-off (mm) for R. Thames at Teddington (1883-1972)

only the 50% value (often written as the P50 value) is to find the average of the 16%, 50% and 84% values. This may be written in the form:

$$\frac{P16 + P50 + P84}{3}$$

From figure 63 the actual values can be inserted giving:

$$\frac{P16 + P50 + P84}{3} = \frac{172 + 246 + 328}{3} = \frac{746}{3} = 248.7 \text{ mm}$$

To check whether it is a better estimate of the mean than the P50 value alone (i.e. 246 mm), the annual run-off of all the 90 years' records can be averaged. This gives the true mean as 248.1 mm.

*Standard deviation*
To give the average value alone as an indication of the run-off of any river basin does not give a very complete picture. It does not indicate how typical the mean value is of any one year's run-off. In figure 60, three examples of normal distribution curves are shown, each with the same mean value, but whereas in figure 60a all years have run-

73

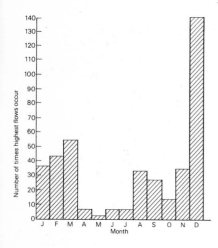

**64** Months in which highest recorded flows for rivers in Great Britain have occurred

offs close to the mean, this is less true of the curve in figure 60b, and the mean value would give very little indication of any year's run-off if they ranged in value as in figure 60c.

An additional indication is thus needed of the way in which values range about the mean. One measure of this is the **standard deviation** which is illustrated in figure 60b. Within one standard deviation of the mean lie 68.26% of all the values. The symbol representing standard deviation is $\sigma$ and its magnitude can be quickly found from a cumulative probability graph. The 84% (P84) and 16% (P16) values are read off the curve and then:

$$\text{standard deviation } (\sigma) = \frac{P84 - P16}{2}$$

Using the values from figure 63 for the annual run-off of the River Thames, gives:

$$\sigma = \frac{328 - 172}{2} = 78 \text{ mm}$$

The mean value was found to be 248 mm, so it can now be said that 68.26% of the annual values lie within the range 248 ± 78 mm, that is between 170 mm and 326 mm. This is quite a wide range, being more than half the value of the mean itself. A narrower distribution about the mean, such as that illustrated in figure 60a, would of course have a smaller standard deviation.

From figure 60b we see that 95% of the values lie within two standard deviations of the mean, that is in the range 248 ± (2 × 78) mm, and 99.73% lie within three standard deviations of the mean.

The mean and the standard deviation together provide figures for comparing any data which vary evenly about an average. For instance river flows in different climates could be compared, the standard deviation giving a measure of the probability of obtaining run-off amounts close to the mean values. It would be found in this case that in drier climates there is a wide dispersion, indicating less reliability of the amount of run-off than in temperate areas.

## Seasonal variability of flows

It has been shown that annual flows vary normally about a mean value, assuming that climate and other factors influencing run-off have not changed. Similarly run-off for any particular month will vary evenly about the mean value for that month as measured over a number of years. The run-off for different months, however, cannot be compared in this way since factors do not operate uniformly from month to month. The same holds for daily discharges. But flooding in particular may result from a particularly high single day's flow. How may its occurrence be predicted?

Figure 64, compiled from the *Surface Water Year Book*, shows for each month the number of river basins in Great Britain which have their highest recorded flow in that month. It indicates the dominance of the month of December, a month of high rainfall following rainy months during which the moisture level in the soil has been restored to field capacity. Figure 65 shows the River Severn in flood at this time. December is also a month when in some areas soils may become frozen, thereby reducing infiltration and giving more rapid run-off, but this effect is more likely in

**65** A stretch of about 3 km along the River Severn in flood during December 1965. The view is south of Shrewsbury, near Wroxeter (looking downstream from SJ562075). The amount of surface water indicates how far the saturated ground extends

**66** Floods on R. Trent at Alrewas, Staffordshire (SK167155). The extent of flooding across the valley floor, which is about 1½ km wide here, can be clearly seen

February and March as is the occurrence of snow. Snow thaw, which is frequently brought about by rain, presumably plays a prominent part in the secondary peak month of March. A regional breakdown of the figures would reveal the dominance of east coast rivers with peak flows in March and February, endorsing the likelihood of this, for snow is more likely to linger in the catchment areas of Britain's east coast rivers. Figure 66 shows the extent of flooding by the River Trent at Alrewas, Staffordshire on 29 March 1955. This followed heavy rain on the 25th and 26th, when Birmingham received 45 mm of rain in 24 hours. Much of Birmingham's run-off enters headwaters of the River Trent and in this case must have contributed considerably to the river's discharge.

The third peak occurs in August and September, months when the incidence of storms is high. Detailed regional analysis of the figures would show that this peak occurs particularly in rivers in southern Scotland where relief and shallow soils may promote rapid run-off.

Summer rainfalls may often be severe and the top four records in Great Britain for falls in a day are on summer days:

| | |
|---|---|
| 18 July 1955 Martinstown, Dorset | 279 mm |
| 28 June 1917 Bruton, Somerset | 243 mm |
| 18 August 1924 Cannington, Somerset | 239 mm |
| 15 August 1952 Simonsbath, Devon | 231 mm |

The last produced the Lynton and Lynmouth disaster which has been well documented.

Clearly then, seasonal variations affect the likelihood of flooding. In certain months, varying regionally although in general December predominates, there is a greater chance of floods occurring. Droughts, generally longer lasting, also vary seasonally. For both, however, knowing in which months they are likely to occur is not enough for planning purposes. One needs to know how likely and how severe they may be in any year, or over a number of years. This may be accomplished by preparing a **flow duration curve**, also known as a **discharge frequency curve**.

*Discharge frequency curve*
Figure 67 is a discharge frequency curve for the River Windrush at Newbridge, Oxfordshire. It shows all the discharges of the river and the percentage of time each was equalled or exceeded. Again, the curved line is less useful than if it were straight, especially at its extremities where it indicates floods and droughts. Plotting the same figures on normal probability paper, used in figure 63, would not straighten the line because of the large range of discharges occurring in the river. To enable it to be plotted easily the axis is divided logarithmically and the resulting line, shown in figure 68, is much closer to a straight line.

Records for the daily flow of a river over at least 5 years, and preferably for much longer, are required to produce a discharge frequency curve. The flows are then grouped into classes, as shown in table 22. The class divisions used here are logarithmically approximately equal in size so that there is fairly even spacing of readings along the frequency curve. Each cumulative total (m) is expressed as a percentage of one more than the overall total number (n) of

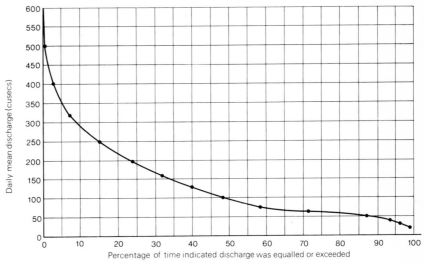

**67** Discharge frequency curve for R. Windrush at Newbridge (1950-60)

**68** Discharge frequency curve for R. Windrush at Newbridge (1950-60) plotted on normal probability paper

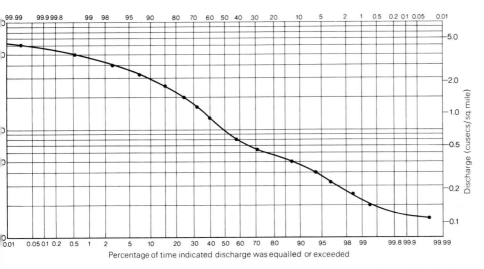

Percentage of time indicated discharge was equalled or exceeded

Table 22    *Discharge frequencies of R. Windrush at Newbridge, Oxfordshire, 1950−60*

| Daily mean discharge in cusecs | 1950−1 | 1951−2 | 1952−3 | 1953−4 | 1954−5 | 1955−6 | 1956−7 | 1957−8 | 1958−9 | 1959−60 | Total 1950−60 | Cumulative total (m) | Plotting position $\frac{m}{n+1} \times 100\%$ |
|---|---|---|---|---|---|---|---|---|---|---|---|---|---|
| 16.1−20 | | | | | | | | | | 27 | 27 | 27 | 0.74 |
| 20.1−25 | | | | | | | | | 4 | 30 | 34 | 61 | 1.67 |
| 25.1−32 | | | | | | 44 | | | 22 | 13 | 79 | 140 | 3.83 |
| 32.1−40 | | | | | | 24 | 36 | | 29 | 11 | 100 | 240 | 6.57 |
| 40.1−50 | | 26 | 13 | 20 | 5 | 51 | 75 | | 30 | 13 | 233 | 473 | 12.9 |
| 50.1−63 | 73 | 100 | 78 | 80 | 21 | 82 | 71 | 18 | 25 | 40 | 588 | 1061 | 29.0 |
| 63.1−79 | 50 | 13 | 87 | 91 | 66 | 22 | 21 | 63 | 16 | 49 | 478 | 1539 | 42.1 |
| 79.1−100 | 21 | 16 | 39 | 60 | 16 | 73 | 43 | 54 | 3 | 30 | 355 | 1894 | 51.8 |
| 100.1−130 | 20 | 26 | 40 | 48 | 24 | 29 | 33 | 56 | 2 | 37 | 315 | 2209 | 60.5 |
| 130.1−160 | 14 | 36 | 35 | 19 | 64 | 13 | 21 | 20 | 14 | 32 | 268 | 2477 | 67.8 |
| 160.1−200 | 30 | 65 | 25 | 23 | 50 | 8 | 23 | 23 | 21 | 25 | 293 | 2770 | 75.8 |
| 200.1−250 | 38 | 40 | 21 | 21 | 56 | 6 | 18 | 53 | 61 | 29 | 343 | 3113 | 85.2 |
| 250.1−320 | 51 | 22 | 19 | 3 | 29 | 12 | 16 | 40 | 79 | 14 | 285 | 3398 | 93.0 |
| 320.1−400 | 44 | 20 | 8 | | 13 | 2 | 7 | 23 | 37 | 8 | 162 | 3560 | 97.4 |
| 400.1−500 | 21 | 2 | | | 16 | | 1 | 13 | 13 | 8 | 74 | 3634 | 99.45 |
| 500.1−630 | 3 | | | | 5 | | | 2 | 9 | | 19 | 3653 | 100.00 |
| Total | 365 | 366 | 365 | 365 | 365 | 366 | 365 | 365 | 365 | 366 | n = 3653 | | |

Table 23    *Discharge frequencies of daily mean flows on R. Glen at Kirknewton, Northumberland 1969–71*

| Mean flow (cusecs) | Frequency of days | Cumulative totals (m) |
|---|---|---|
| 0.2513–0.3981 | 21 | 21 |
| 0.3982–0.6310 | 239 | 260 |
| 0.6311–1.0 | 183 | 443 |
| 1.01–1.585 | 132 | 575 |
| 1.586–2.512 | 159 | 734 |
| 2.513–3.981 | 133 | 867 |
| 3.982–6.310 | 118 | 985 |
| 6.311–10.0 | 60 | 1045 |
| 10.01–15.85 | 36 | 1081 |
| 15.86–25.12 | 9 | 1090 |
| 25.13–39.81 | 2 | 1092 |
| 39.82–63.10 | 3 | 1095 |

Table 24    *Annual maximum daily flows of R. Avon at Bath, Somerset (used in the construction of the Bath flood prevention scheme)*

| Year | Flow (cumecs) | Rank (M) | $\dfrac{M}{n+1}$ | Plotting position % (probability of each flow occurring) |
|---|---|---|---|---|
| 1941 | 97.7 | 21 | 0.8077 | 80.77 |
| 1942 | 76.5 | 24 | 0.9230 | 92.30 |
| 1943 | 134.8 | 14 | 0.5384 | 53.84 |
| 1944 | – | – | – | – |
| 1945 | 106.5 | 18.5 | 0.7115 | 71.15 |
| 1946 | 172.8 | 7 | 0.2692 | 26.92 |
| 1947 | 277.5 | 3 | 0.1154 | 11.54 |
| 1948 | – | – | – | – |
| 1949 | 82.1 | 22.5 | 0.8654 | 86.54 |
| 1950 | 196.8 | 5 | 0.1923 | 19.23 |
| 1951 | – | – | – | – |
| 1952 | 106.5 | 18.5 | 0.7115 | 71.15 |
| 1953 | 61.7 | 25 | 0.9615 | 96.15 |
| 1954 | 183.2 | 6 | 0.2308 | 23.08 |
| 1955 | 160.7 | 9 | 0.3461 | 34.61 |
| 1956 | 108.5 | 17 | 0.6538 | 65.38 |
| 1957 | 101.1 | 20 | 0.7692 | 76.92 |
| 1958 | 127.4 | 15 | 0.5769 | 57.69 |
| 1959 | 163.7 | 8 | 0.3077 | 30.77 |
| 1960 | 283.2 | 2 | 0.0769 | 7.69 |
| 1961 | 135.9 | 13 | 0.5000 | 50.00 |
| 1962 | 116.4 | 16 | 0.6154 | 61.54 |
| 1963 | 259.1 | 4 | 0.1538 | 15.38 |
| 1964 | 82.1 | 22.5 | 0.8654 | 86.54 |
| 1965 | 146.6 | 10 | 0.3846 | 38.46 |
| 1966 | 140.6 | 12 | 0.4615 | 46.15 |
| 1967 | 146.2 | 11 | 0.4231 | 42.31 |
| 1968 | 286.8 | 1 | 0.0385 | 3.85 |

Number of values (n) = 25

Mean $Q_{a\,max.}$ = 150.20 cumecs

**69** Discharge frequency curves for
selected rivers in Great Britain

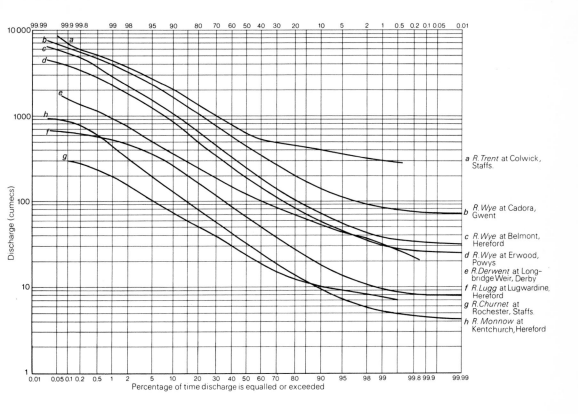

a R. Trent at Colwick,
Staffs.

b R. Wye at Cadora,
Gwent

c R. Wye at Belmont,
Hereford

d R. Wye at Erwood,
Powys
e R. Derwent at Long-
bridge Weir, Derby
f R. Lugg at Lugwardine,
Hereford
g R. Churnet at
Rochester, Staffs.
h R. Monnow at
Kentchurch, Hereford

readings used. This gives the plotting position shown in the last
column of table 22.

Table 23 is a summary of 3 years' daily mean discharges of the
River Glen at Kirknewton in Northumberland. It can be used to
produce a discharge frequency curve if tracing paper is placed over
figure 69 and the axis numbered appropriately in cycles of 0.1 to
1.0, 1.0 to 10.0 and 10.0 to 100.0.

Discharge frequency curves plotted to the same scale can be useful ways of comparing the characteristics of different drainage basins
as they are reflected in the river flow. The relative position of the
curves in figure 69 signifies their relative discharges, that of the River
Churnet being the least and that of the Trent the largest. A curve
with a steep slope throughout shows a highly variable stream, whilst
a flatter slope indicates a slower response to rainfall. The three rivers
in the Trent basin (a, e and g) show a slower response than those of
the Wye basin (b, c, d, f and h), perhaps an indication of the impermeable rocks, greater relief, steeper slopes and, in general, shallower
soils of the latter catchments. The curves give a broad indication of
the overall movement of water through the basin and may be used in
conjunction with chapter 4 to examine the factors which control
movements in each basin. The slope of the lower end of a frequency
curve reflects periods of low flows and shows the effect of storage,
either in the soil or as groundwater. Large storage amounts, giving a
significant baseflow, will tend to flatten the lower end of the curve
as in the case of the Trent and Churnet in particular. River basins
which receive a lot of snow or are swampy during the wet seasons

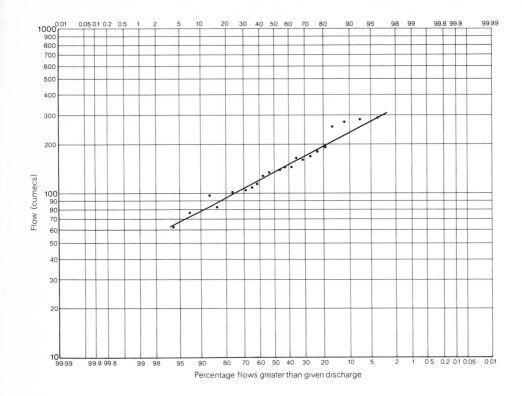

store water in these ways and tend to have a flat slope at the upper
end of the curve. The same effect is produced in streams with large
flood-plain storage and this is the cause of the flattening at the upper
end of the Lugg curve. The valley below Leominster (on the River
Lugg, some 25 km upstream from Lugwardine) is noted for extensive flooding, often two or three times a year.

Such curves are obviously of great value in analysing the range of
flows for a river. However, to analyse specifically for flood or
drought frequency more detail at either end of the curve is ideally
required, and frequently these data are more easily obtainable than
those for the whole range of flows for a river.

*Maximum flow probability*
A method for recording daily maximum flows using a stage pole was
described in chapter 2, and these data can be used to calculate probable frequencies of each magnitude of maximum flow. Naturally for
recording flooding it is the maximum daily flow, rather than the
mean flow for that day, which is required. The largest peaks, or all
flows above a certain magnitude, are recorded each year, as in table
24, which gives the maximum daily flow recorded each year from
1941–68 on the River Avon in Bath, England. A probability curve
can be drawn up by ranking the 25 years in order of their maximum
daily discharge (M), as in the third column. The plotting position
(P) on the probability scale is calculated, as before, using the
formula:

$$P = \frac{M}{n+1} \times 100\%$$

**1** Annual maximum daily flow (m.g.d.) of
. Thames at Teddington (1883-1972)

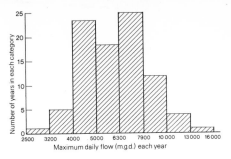

where n is the total number of values (25 in this case). This gives the probability of each flow occurring. Thus the probability of the largest flow (286.8 cumecs) occurring is $1/26 = .0385$ or 3.85%, i.e. 3.85 flows out of 100 will be equal to or greater than the largest value of the 25 year period. The probability of a flow less than the largest is $1 - P = 1 - 0.0385$ or 96.15%.

Figure 70 shows the plot of the data for the River Avon and can be used to obtain the probabilities of flows other than those given in the fourth column of table 24. From it we can find that the mean maximum daily discharge per annum, that is the 50% value, is 135.9 cumecs.

*Recurrence interval*
Another useful piece of information that can be derived is the return period or **recurrence interval** (in years) of any particular size of flow. This period is given by:

$$\text{Recurrence interval} = \frac{1}{P} \text{ or } \frac{n+1}{M}$$

Thus from table 24 the recurrence interval of a maximum daily flow equal to or greater than the largest which occurred is:

$$\frac{1}{P} = \frac{1}{0.0385} = 25.91 \text{ years}$$

The mean of all the annual maximum flows found by summing the annual discharges and by dividing by n is 150.26 cumecs. Figure 70 shows that this has a probable recurrence of about 39% or 0.39. The recurrence interval, being $1/P$, is therefore $1/0.39$ or 2.56 years.

It has been found by study of data from many river gauging stations that once in every 2.33 years on average the highest flow of the year will equal or exceed the mean of the annual floods over a long period. Ideally, the data for all high flows (above an arbitrarily fixed level) should be used, if they are available, to calculate flood recurrence intervals and produce a **partial-duration curve**. However, it has been found that recurrence intervals calculated from all high flows and those calculated using annual maximum flows (preferably actual maximums and not maximum mean daily flow) are approximately equal for records of 10 years or longer. The value of 2.56 which we calculated above is not far from the average of 2.33 found by the other method. Since maximum annual flows are more readily available than all high flows they are more convenient to use.

In using statistical sampling of this kind a minimum of thirty values is generally regarded as necessary. Since flood flows do not occur strictly by chance, to achieve the same variability in the data as would occur in chance or random occurrences, an even larger number of values, between 60 and 100, is ideally required, but rarely available.

Figure 71 shows the distribution (on a logarithmic scale) of maxi-

Table 25    *Annual maximum daily natural flow of R. Thames at Teddington (m.g.d.)*

| Year | Flow | Year | Flow | Year | Flow |
|------|------|------|------|------|------|
| 1883 | 9 703 | 1917 | 4 441 | 1951 | 7 313 |
| 1884 | 4 390 | 1918 | 6 663 | 1952 | 5 004 |
| 1885 | 4 641 | 1919 | 6 352 | 1953 | 4 353 |
| 1886 | 4 561 | 1920 | 4 768 | 1954 | 8 603 |
| 1887 | 5 394 | 1921 | 4 561 | 1955 | 7 125 |
| 1888 | 4 001 | 1922 | 3 760 | 1956 | 5 999 |
| 1889 | 4 512 | 1923 | 4 398 | 1957 | 5 970 |
| 1890 | 3 888 | 1924 | 6 506 | 1958 | 6 017 |
| 1891 | 6 451 | 1925 | 9 919 | 1959 | 7 123 |
| 1892 | 4 487 | 1926 | 7 031 | 1960 | 8 664 |
| 1893 | 5 696 | 1927 | 8 631 | 1961 | 7 189 |
| 1894 | 15 000 | 1928 | 9 999 | 1962 | 6 542 |
| 1895 | 5 782 | 1929 | 10 489 | 1963 | 6 538 |
| 1896 | 4 390 | 1930 | 6 292 | 1964 | 7 018 |
| 1897 | 6 668 | 1931 | 4 264 | 1965 | 5 041 |
| 1898 | 3 575 | 1932 | 5 216 | 1966 | 6 151 |
| 1899 | 4 981 | 1933 | 9 095 | 1967 | 5 945 |
| 1900 | 10 136 | 1934 | 3 778 | 1968 | 11 404 |
| 1901 | 3 811 | 1935 | 6 453 | 1969 | 6 325 |
| 1902 | 2 954 | 1936 | 9 088 | 1970 | 4 675 |
| 1903 | 7 335 | 1937 | 8 321 | 1971 | 6 886 |
| 1904 | 9 817 | 1938 | 4 541 | 1972 | 6 273 |
| 1905 | 4 361 | 1939 | 7 021 | | |
| 1906 | 4 734 | 1940 | 7 784 | | |
| 1907 | 7 140 | 1941 | 6 500 | | |
| 1908 | 6 310 | 1942 | 5 670 | | |
| 1909 | 4 335 | 1943 | 8 685 | | |
| 1910 | 8 134 | 1944 | 4 959 | | |
| 1911 | 5 151 | 1945 | 4 878 | | |
| 1912 | 6 970 | 1946 | 6 833 | | |
| 1913 | 4 852 | 1947 | 13 572 | | |
| 1914 | 5 763 | 1948 | 4 323 | | |
| 1915 | 11 119 | 1949 | 5 679 | | |
| 1916 | 7 098 | 1950 | 6 162 | | |

mum daily natural flows of the River Thames at Teddington for the years 1883 to 1972. It is evident that they are not far from being normally distributed, which is why the methods described above can be used. The curve is not even, being slightly off-centre or **skewed**, and for best results paper specially prepared for plotting such skewed distributions and known as Gumbel paper should be used. However, logarithmic probability paper as in figure 70 is adequate to demonstrate the method, and gives quite good approximation.

Table 25 gives the actual maximum daily flows of the River Thames each year from 1883 to 1972 and may be used for plotting the maximum daily discharge probabilities if tracing paper is placed over figure 70 and the numbering of the axis changed to show the range from 1000 to 10 000 to 100 000 million gallons per day.

## Data collection

It was shown in chapter 2 that it is difficult to measure discharge once banks have overflowed. Discontinuities in the stage/discharge curve above bank-full flows make readings above this level less precise than for smaller flows. Consequently on days when high flows occur authorities make every attempt to record them by all means possible. Such difficulties, together with the limited length of most flow records, make flood recurrence prediction less precise than it would be under ideal conditions. The importance of high flows, in eroding the channel and banks and in transporting sediment, will be shown in the next chapter.

## Economic aspects of extreme flows

As abstraction of water from rivers for public water supply increases so the **minimum acceptable flow (m.a.f.)** increases. A more important consideration than volume, however, in setting a minimum acceptable flow in a river, is often the pollutant level. Public use of water and effluent discharge do not vary seasonally in the way that river flows do, so the ratio of effluent to river water increases in summer months when flows are low. This produces a very great strain upon the water's available bacteria, which break down most pollutants and render them less harmful, and it sets a minimum level of possible dilution. There are two possible remedies – to increase summer flows by storing water from winter rainfall, and to reduce pollutant levels.

The latter is difficult as it often means tracing the offending polluter, and usually proving he is to blame. Both methods undoubtedly have to be used. The former has the advantage that reservoirs built to store water for supplementing summer flows, (termed **compensating reservoirs**, as opposed to **direct supply** reservoirs), can also be used to take some winter run-off when the river might otherwise flood. The amounts that can be drawn off from peak discharges are usually small, however, since reservoirs are generally in upland areas and only on one of many tributaries, all of which are supplying run-off to a major river. Unless reservoirs are put on many tributaries flood protection can only be slight. In addition waters at flood times are often highly charged with sediment. Sediment settling to the bottom of the reservoir can fill it within a few decades. This is discussed further in chapter 8.

Flood control therefore also involves maintenance of the channel by regular clearance of weeds and dredging to speed run-off, and construction of flood embankments. Flood embankments are often set back from the river channel giving additional channel space for high flows, as in the Washlands between the old and new Bedford levels in the fenlands of England. Deliberately allowing land to be flooded is justified to reduce the danger of overtopping of the embankments by very high flows. Nevertheless it may not be always possible or economically viable to completely 'flood-proof' a river's course. The cost of embanking against a flood with a recurrence interval of 50 years may be far more than double the cost of containing a 25 year flood. If the damage caused is only twice as much then it is clearly uneconomic to build defences for the 50 year flood.

There is a great danger on the part of people unfamiliar with the magnitude/recurrence relationships and the economics of flood protection, to assume that flood 'protection' is against *all* possibilities of flooding. Similarly, to safeguard against all possible drought conditions does not make economic sense. Yet in many countries the population regard water supply as a 'right' and shortages come as a shock. This was illustrated during the exceptional drought conditions of 1976 in Britain. To have installed adequate storage of water to meet a drought, with a recurrence interval of perhaps less than once every 250 years, would have meant spending vast sums of money relative to such an infrequent need.

Perceptions of flood and drought are providing interesting research areas for geographers. The 1976 drought followed in winter by quite extensive flooding on a number of occasions will certainly have changed British perceptions.

### Selected references

McCullagh, P. 1974. *Data Use and Interpretation*. Oxford: OUP.

Newson, M.D. 1975. *Flooding and Flood Hazard in the UK*. Oxford: OUP.

UNESCO. 1969. Discharges of selected rivers of the world. *UNESCO Studies and Reports in Hydrology*, No. 5.

Water Resources Board. 1970. Logarithmic plotting of stage—discharge operations. *Technical Note 3*.

# 8

# River load

In most areas of the world the products of weathering and erosion
are removed from the drainage basin by rivers and streams. The
material carried by rivers is termed **load**. It is possible to divide load
into three types:

(1) bed load;
(2) suspended sediment load;
(3) solution or solute load.

Bed load and suspended sediment are composed of 'solid' material
and are sometimes collectively referred to as **particulate load**. The
minimum diameter of particulate material is about half a **micron**
(i.e. about 0.0005 mm). The solution, or solute, load is in true
chemical solution in the same fashion as salt in sea water.

The three-fold division is in some ways unsatisfactory as small
particles can act as bed load when river velocities are low, but as
river velocity increases the same particles can be lifted from the
stream bed and become transported as suspended load. However,
most workers in this field recognise the three types listed above.

## Sediment transport and velocity

It is important to consider the velocity necessary to move particulate
material of different sizes. In a general sense, as would be expected,
the faster the river velocity the larger the particles it transports.
However, this is not the case for particles with diameters less than
0.5 mm (classified as medium sand grade). The relationship between
the velocity needed to move the particle (**erosion velocity**) and its
size is illustrated in figure 72. For a particle with a diameter of 1 mm
a velocity of about 25 cm/sec is necessary, and for one of 10 mm
diameter the necessary velocity is approximately 100 cm/sec.

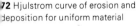

**72** Hjulstrom curve of erosion and
deposition for uniform material

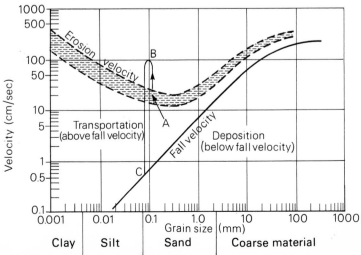

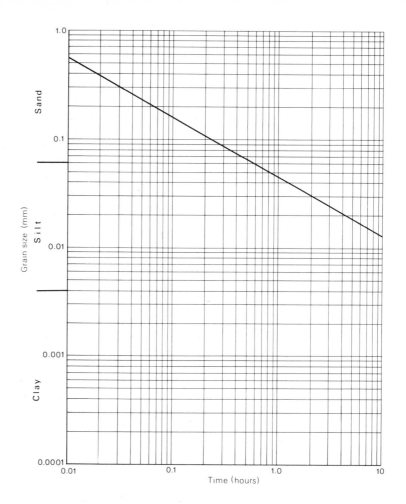

**73** Approximate settling time for particles of differing grain size

For particles smaller than about 0.5 mm the velocity required for erosion to occur needs to increase as grain size decreases. For example, a silt particle with a diameter of 0.01 mm requires an erosion velocity of about 70 cm/sec, which is nearly three times greater than for a sand particle with a diameter one hundred times larger. Erosion velocity is represented by a large band, because other factors such as the shape of the channel bed also influence whether particles are picked up or not. These results were first described from laboratory experiments in the 1930s and the graph in figure 72 is often referred to as the **Hjulstrom curve**, after a pioneer worker on sediments. The reason for the rather unexpected behaviour of the smaller grains is that they are bound together by electrical bonding, and also that stream channels composed of such small particles are normally smooth with no protruding grains. Stream channels composed of coarse particles, say boulders, offer a larger surface area on which the turbulent flow of the stream can act.

Figure 72 also illustrates another feature which is important for particulate load transport. Once the erosion velocity has been reached small particles tend to move as suspended load. For a particle with a diameter of 0.1 mm erosion velocity is about 30 cm/sec and once this velocity is exceeded the particle starts to move (point

A on figure 72). Let us assume, for the sake of illustration, that the particle is picked up by water moving at 100 cm/sec at which stage it is moving as suspended load (point B on figure 72). Subsequently the particle moves into water with a lower velocity, less than the erosion velocity curve. Small particles of this kind do not then settle onto the bottom of the stream channel but remain in transport until the lower line of the curve, the **fall velocity**, is reached. This is marked as point C on the diagram. A particle with a diameter of 0.1 mm will remain in transport until the velocity falls to about 0.8 cm/sec. In summary, a 0.1 mm particle will remain at rest on the bottom until a velocity of 30 cm/sec is attained (point A), and it will then continue in motion until the velocity decreases to the fall velocity, C on the diagram.

For larger particles, however, the difference between the erosion velocity and the fall (or settling) velocity is negligible. This at least matches experience and is the same basic principle as stirring up a mixture of sediment in a jam jar. The coarse particles settle almost immediately after stirring ceases, while the fine particles will remain in suspension for many hours. The approximate settling times for particles of different sizes is given in figure 73.

It cannot be overstressed that the Hjulstrom curve is based upon laboratory flume experiments and that the field situation is very much more complex. Despite this restriction it is an instructive exercise to measure the size of material in a stream channel, especially after a flood, and to obtain an estimate of the velocities necessary to move the material by using the Hjulstrom curve. The Hjulstrom curve also explains why most river flood plains are composed of fine grained sediment with a low fall velocity, and usually lack coarse grained material. As a river goes over its banks (exceeds bank-full conditions) the velocity usually decreases and large diameter material is almost immediately deposited, whilst the finer material continues to be transported and spreads more widely over the flood plain. Erosion velocities necessary to move material are much higher than those normally encountered in streams under normal flow conditions. For an example compare the velocities on the Hjulstrom curve to the point velocity values given in figure 4a. Figure 4a shows a fast flowing stream with a steep gradient under normal flow conditions.

It is against the background of the Hjulstrom curve that we can consider particulate material, either as bed load or suspended load.

## Bed load

Material that moves as bed load remains in contact with the bed of the stream and moves by a combination of rolling, sliding and slipping. Bed load is, without doubt, the most difficult form of load on which to make measurements. The difficulty is that the particles usually only move at times of high stage (river level) when the velocity at the bottom of the river channel is great. We have already seen in chapter 2 that it is very difficult to measure the velocity of a stream near to its bed and such difficulties are greatest at times of flood. It is also difficult, in practice, to measure the bed load that is transported over any given time period. There are three possible methods that can be employed to measure or obtain estimates of the bed load passing a given point in a river channel. These are:

(1) bed load traps;
(2) measurement of material held up behind artificial structures;
(3) marked pebbles.

*Bed load traps*
Bed load traps can only be effectively used on small streams and consist of a simple box inserted into the river channel and sometimes covered by a grid. The box must be placed so that its top is level with the floor of the channel. After a period of time the material is collected from the box and measured both for the size of the particles involved and the total weight. Results obtained from a simple bed load trap of this kind are given in Gregory and Walling (1971). Movement is not continuous and is confined to periods of flood discharge. Such techniques are only practical on small streams and the construction and emplacement is more difficult than the description given above may suggest.

*Material trapped behind artificial structures*
The principle can be illustrated by reference to work on dam design. When a dam is constructed the shape and size of the lake to be formed behind the dam is accurately surveyed so the volume of water to be stored will be known precisely. Repeated surveys of the floor of the lake, after a dam is complete, demonstrate that sedimentation takes place and such sedimentation reduces the storage volume behind the dam. In fact the rate of sedimentation is one of the most important quantities that needs to be known before a dam is constructed because it is this quantity that determines the useful life of the dam.

It must be remembered that the material deposited in the reservoir behind a dam is composed of the bed load *plus* a proportion of the suspended sediment. This is because the rate of water movement in the reservoir is very slow compared to that of the input rivers.

A study of sedimentation behind a dam has been made recently for a small dam in the Kisongo Reservoir in northern Tanzania. The dam was completed in 1960 and is fed by rivers draining a catchment area of 9.3 $km^2$. The maximum capacity of the reservoir as first built was 120 000 $m^3$ and a survey of the original bottom topography is given in figure 74a. Sedimentation was rapid and a survey of the bottom in October 1969 showed that 31% of the original capacity had been lost due to the deposition of material in the reservoir behind the dam. A further survey in October 1971, illustrated in figure 74b, established that the initial capacity had been reduced by a total of 40%. Figure 75 is a long profile of the dam showing silting up in the periods 1960–9 and 1969–71. There is evidence that the rate of sedimentation has been increasing and it is likely that one of the major factors responsible is that the water supply afforded by the reservoir has led to an increase in the number of cattle in its neighbourhood and this in turn has accelerated the rate of soil erosion. The material eroded is carried by sheetwash into the streams and thus to the reservoir so that its capacity is lost at a progressively increasing rate.

The amount of material deposited in the reservoir gives a sediment yield for the whole catchment area of 481 $m^3/km^2/year$, or

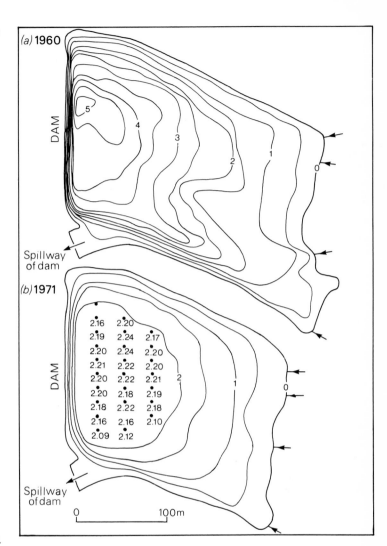

**74** The bottom topography of the Kisongo Reservoir, Tanzania, as shown in the original survey (1960) and 11 years later

*(a)* **1960**

DAM

5
4
3
2
1
0

Spillway
of dam

*(b)* **1971**

DAM

| 2.16 | 2.20 | |
| 2.19 | 2.24 | 2.17 |
| 2.20 | 2.24 | 2.20 |
| 2.21 | 2.22 | 2.20 |
| 2.20 | 2.22 | 2.21 |
| 2.20 | 2.18 | 2.19 |
| 2.18 | 2.22 | 2.18 |
| 2.16 | 2.16 | 2.10 |
| 2.09 | 2.12 | |

2
1
0

Spillway
of dam

0       100m

**75** Long profiles of the Kisongo Reservoir, Tanzania, showing sedimentation

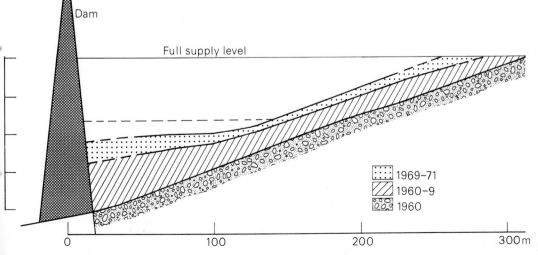

Dam

Full supply level

1969–71
1960–9
1960

0      100      200      300m

89

Particulate load, incorporating all the bed load, for small streams can be collected in a similar way by damming a stream. A weir similar to that illustrated in figure 10 can be used to obtain an estimate of bed load. The simplest method is to line the pool behind the weir with a sheet of heavy gauge polythene which is fixed to the weir plate itself. After a period, which includes a time of high discharge, the sheet can be carefully lifted and the material measured.

expressed in other units an overall surface lowering rate of approximately 0.5 mm/year. These overall erosion rates are very high indeed and under natural vegetation conditions the rate would probably be only a hundredth of this.

A section taken through the sediments shows them to be composed of a number of individual layers or laminations. Each lamination starts with coarse sediment and grades upwards into progressively finer material, and represents the sediment brought into the reservoir after each major flood. Once the sediment-laden water reaches the reservoir the velocity is reduced and the sediment settles out, the coarser material sinking to the bottom first. Each major dry season is marked by a particularly thick layer of very fine material, which needs a long period of time to settle out (see figure 73).

*Marked pebbles*
We have already discussed the relationship between particle size and the velocity of the stream necessary for the particle to move as illustrated by the Hjulstrom curve (figure 72). It was stressed that the curve was obtained from flume studies and that the situation under field conditions is more complex. In addition to the velocity of the stream the following factors also affect the movement of particles as bed load: the density of the material forming the particle, the shape (which determines the surface area exposed to stream flow) and the nature of the stream channel on which the particle is resting. Clearly if a particle, such as a small pebble, is resting on a smooth rock surface it will move at lower stream velocities than an identical pebble packed between other pebbles.

It is possible to indicate the importance of the various controlling factors by the use of marked pebbles. The pebbles can either be placed on the stream bed and re-located after a period of high stage conditions, or pebbles of differing weights, sizes and shapes can be added to a fast flowing stream to establish what are the limiting cases for movement to occur.

Pebbles added to a stream prior to high discharge are best painted with distinctive colours and perhaps numbered. Pebbles of different sizes from, say, 1 cm to 10 or 20 cm on the long axis are placed on the stream bed, for instance in a line across the

channel. The weights of individual pebbles and their position on the stream bed should be noted. After a period of high stage, note which pebbles have moved and try to find their new position. If this experiment is attempted it is essential that the pebbles are placed in a stream where they will not be disturbed by inquisitive visitors picking them up!

A variant of this exercise can be undertaken by adding a size-graded series of pebbles to a stream until the critical grade is found when the river flow starts to move the pebbles. The exercise is more successful if the pebbles are added to a smooth surface, for instance a smooth metal

plate. The plate is placed on the bottom of the stream channel, initially in a horizontal position. The measured pebbles are added one at a time until movement is observed. The experiment can be repeated with the plate inclined at different angles. By using pebbles of differing shapes and weights and by varying the inclination of the plate the controls on the movement of the bed load can be demonstrated. Naturally for the experiment to be a success a shallow stream is required with a relatively fast flow and the smaller the pebbles used the better are the results.

*Conclusions*
The literature on river bed load is very sparse and only the most general comments can be made on the amount of material transported in this manner. Bed load movement of large particles occurs only rarely but when conditions are suitable the total weight of material moved can be very considerable. It is interesting in Britain to speculate whether the large boulders frequently observed in moun-

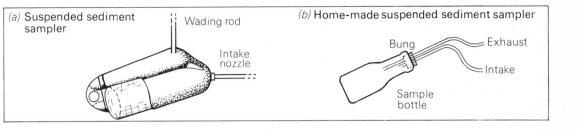

Wading rod

Intake nozzle

(b) Home-made suspended sediment sampler

Bung — Exhaust

— Intake

Sample bottle

tain streams have actually been transported by the rivers themselves or whether they were originally moved by glacial action or mass movement and have remained in the same position for a long time. There is little doubt, however, that in times of exceptional flood very large boulders can be moved. Research has shown that for lowland rivers it is unusual for more than 10% of the particulate load to be transported as bed load and frequently the figure is less than 5%.

## Suspended sediment load

The finer material carried by rivers can be transported fully suspended, with no direct contact with the floor of the river channel. This distinguishes suspended load from bed load. There is a subdivision, **saltation load**. Particles moving by saltation tend to proceed downstream in a series of 'hopping' movements. By convention for fluvial studies saltation load is included with suspended load, the reason being that the method of measurement normally used for suspended load also includes saltation load. The division of material moved by fluvial action into bed load (continuous contact with the bottom of the stream), suspended load (weight of the particles borne by the water) and saltation load are exactly comparable to the movement of particulate material by wind action in arid regions.

### Measurement of suspended load

The instruments for obtaining samples for suspended sediment analysis are of American design. The simplest used for small streams consists of a bottle fitted to a sampler with a small nozzle that allows the water to enter at approximately the same velocity as the stream is flowing. A sampler of this type (shown in figure 76a) is used for obtaining **depth integrated samples**. A sample is obtained by slowly lowering the sampler to the bottom of the stream and then raising it to the surface at the same speed; this operation is repeated several times until the bottle is nearly full. The intake nozzle does not in fact sample the lowest few centimetres of the stream as the sediment in this lowest section of the channel is considered to be solely bed load. The sample is transferred to a numbered bottle and returned to the laboratory for analysis. The analysis too is simple and consists of filtering the sample through a filter paper or membrane. The filter paper is weighed dry before filtering, and again after filtering and re-drying. The gain in weight and the volume of the sample enable the amount of the suspended sediment to be obtained. Suspended sediment values are usually expressed in terms of concentration by weight in parts per million, which is the same unit as milligrammes per litre (mg/l). Similar samplers of a

A simple, inexpensive sediment sampler can be constructed using a wide-necked bottle such as a milk bottle and a rubber bung through which two pieces of metal tube are inserted (see figure 76b). The water flows in through one of the tubes and air is expelled from the other. The diameter of the tubes should be about 5 mm. For depth integrated sampling in shallow streams the adapted milk bottle is held in a clamp.

heavier design are used in conjunction with cable-ways or bridges to obtain samples from larger rivers.

The major difficulty encountered in measuring suspended sediment is that the gain in weight on filtering samples collected under stream baseflow conditions is very small, and difficulties occur in accurately determining it. Any type of filter paper is suitable but glass fibre papers are probably best. The filtering is speeded up if the filters are used in combination with a Buchner funnel and a simple vacuum pump. A sample of about 200 ml volume is normally used although, to some extent, the problems of the small gain in weight on filtering are overcome by using a larger volume. Certainly at times of high stage conditions very satisfactory results can be obtained by the use of the simple equipment and methods described above. The calculations are as follows:

$$\frac{\text{Concentration of sediment}}{\text{in mg/l}} = \frac{\text{Weight of residue on filter paper in mg}}{\text{Volume of sample in l}}$$

A visual impression of the amount of suspended sediment can be obtained by filtering a standard quantity of water, say 250 ml, and comparing the colour of the filter papers under differing discharge conditions. It is important that the samples compared are all from the same river site as the colour of the sediment can vary quite markedly from river to river or from site to site on a single river. The filtered water can also be used for measuring solute load, as explained later.

*Suspended sediment concentrations*

We have already stated that suspended sediment increases with discharge at an individual river site and it is useful now to consider actual field results. The results given below are based upon work undertaken on rivers in the Bristol region; the samples were collected under a range of discharge conditions. Figure 77 shows the results for a number of samples collected from the River Avon at Melksham in Wiltshire. Although there is a scatter of points on the diagram a good idea of the relationship of suspended sediment to discharge can be obtained by considering the 'best fit' line drawn through the points. Thus for a discharge of 4 cumecs the suspended sediment concentration approximates to 4 mg/l whilst at 100 cumecs the suspended sediment concentration is 1000 mg/l. However, because flow has increased by twenty-five times and the suspended sediment concentration by two hundred and fifty times, the quantity of material carried as suspended sediment load at bank-full conditions (corresponding to approximately 100 cumecs) is over six thousand times greater than at low flow.

Observations on other rivers show that a similar relationship always exists between suspended sediment and discharge, although the slope of the line will vary.

## Solution or solute load

In addition to particulate load rivers carry material in true chemical solution. For many rivers the quantity of material carried in solution far exceeds that transported in particulate form. The solution load is composed of many differing chemical elements and it is possible

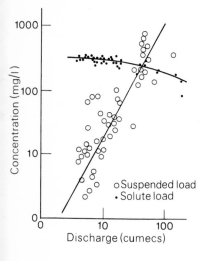

**77** The relationship of suspended sediment and solute concentrations to discharge, R. Avon, Melksham, Wiltshire

to undertake a detailed chemical analysis of the water to obtain information on the concentration of each of the elements involved. However such detailed chemical analyses are time consuming and involve complex analytical methods.

A useful measure of the total solution load, usually referred to as **total dissolved solids**, can be obtained by evaporating to dryness a sample of filtered river water and accurately weighing the solid residue. Unlike suspended sediment samples there is no special procedure for obtaining samples for the determination of solute load; all that is required is a clean bottle which is dipped into the stream. The sample container should be kept stoppered until analysis is undertaken. Evaporating to dryness however, needs considerable care. An accurate balance is also required as the weight of the total dissolved solids is usually very small. A sample of 250 ml or larger should be used.

*Limestone solutional erosion*
Most rocks are composed of a large number of minerals and the chemical composition of the water draining from the area is complex. The major exception is the erosion by solution of limestone and this will be used as an example of the process of **solutional erosion** and the calculation of load. Limestone is chemically a very simple rock type, with calcite the dominant mineral. Calcite is chemically calcium carbonate, $CaCO_3$. Limestones are more susceptible to solutional erosion than other rock types. Indeed, the landforms of limestone regions (such as dry valleys, caves, limestone pavements) are a result of this susceptibility.

In general terms the solution chemistry of limestone is described by the following equation:

$$CaCO_3 + H_2O + CO_2 = Ca(HCO_3)_2$$

Limestone     Water     Carbon dioxide     Calcium bicarbonate

As we see, the calcium is removed in solution as calcium bicarbonate and by analysing water draining from a limestone area for its calcium content the form and rate of the solutional erosion can be assessed. There is a relatively simple chemical titration available to measure the amount of calcium present in natural waters. The method and calculations are described in Rendle, Vokins and Davis. The analysis measures the calcium content of the water but it is usual to present the values in terms of calcium carbonate, expressed as milligrams per litre (mg/l). This quantity is sometimes referred to as 'calcium hardness'. If a laboratory is not available it is possible to purchase 'water hardness' packs with the chemicals already made up to their correct strength (for instance the pack marketed by British Drug Houses (BDH) Limited).

Limestone waters can be monitored to discover how the calcium content varies with discharge. For streams flowing over limestone before disappearing underground the solute content tends to vary inversely with rainfall (and therefore with discharge) which is illustrated by the results in figure 78. For springs in limestone areas the calcium content usually remains constant regardless of variations in discharge, as illustrated in figure 79 for three large springs that emerge around the periphery of the Mendip Hills in Somerset. It would appear that the inverse relationship shown for surface lime-

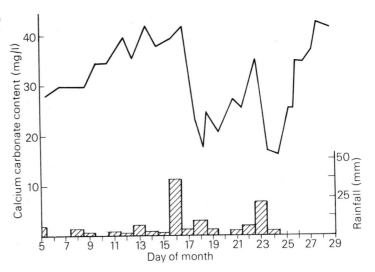

**78** Variations in calcium content with rainfall for a surface limestone stream

Calcium carbonate content (mg/l)

Rainfall (mm)

Day of month

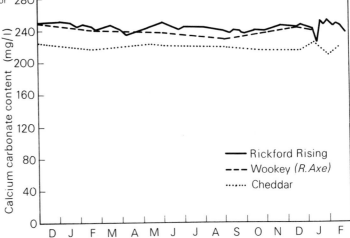

**79** Calcium carbonate content of major Mendip springs, Somerset

Calcium carbonate content (mg/l)

—— Rickford Rising
--- Wookey (R.Axe)
······ Cheddar

To obtain a value for the solution load it is necessary to multiply the concentration by the discharge. For annual figures the load removed would be:

$$L = T_c Q$$

where L is the load removed per year in mg, $T_c$ is the mean annual calcium concentration of the spring in mg/l $CaCO_3$, and Q is the mean annual discharge in litres. In metric tonnes per year this becomes:

$$L = \frac{T_c Q}{10^9}$$

Similar calculations can be made for the load removed over short time periods.

stone streams (figure 78) is related to the speed of throughflow (see chapter 4) through the soil horizons. In time of heavy rainfall the movement is relatively fast and there is little time for the carbon dioxide in the soil water to react with the calcium carbonate, so at times of high stream discharge the calcium concentration is low. Conversely when it has not rained for a period the streams still flow, albeit at baseflow conditions, but the water flowing in the streams is composed of throughflow water that has been in the soil for a longer period. The carbon dioxide in the soil water has thus had a longer period to dissolve a near saturation quantity of calcium. For water emerging at springs in limestone areas (figure 79) it is thought that the bulk of the water has been underground for a reasonable length of time and that saturation conditions between the water, carbon dioxide and the calcium carbonate have been achieved.

## Calculation of erosion rate

To compare the rate of erosion from one limestone region to another it is usual to express the load in terms of the volumes of limestone rock removed. A simple formula to obtain this figure was suggested by Corbel, a French geomorphologist, in the late 1950s. The Corbel equation multiplies the concentration value, $T_c$, by a figure for the mean annual effective run-off (that is rainfall less evapotranspiration). This is less accurate than using the discharge figure Q, but has the advantage that it is easier to obtain values and estimates for mean annual rainfall and evapotranspiration than to obtain discharge values. The product of concentration and effective run-off is divided by the density of the limestone in order to obtain a value for the volume of limestone removed. The density of limestone is usually close to 2.5 $g/cm^3$.

Table 26    *World-wide values for limestone solutional erosion*

| Area | Mean annual precipitation (mm) | Quantity of limestone removed ($m^3/km^2/yr$) |
|---|---|---|
| *Cold climates* | | |
| Somerset Island, N. Canada | 130 | 2 |
| R. Tanana, Central Alaska | 450 | 40 |
| Svartisen, N. Norway | 740–4000 | 275–5000 |
| Vercors, France | 1500–2500 | 240 |
| R. Punkva, Moravia, Czechoslovakia | 620 | 25 |
| *Moist temperate climates* | | |
| R. Fergus and R. Shannon, Ireland | 1000–1250 | 51–53 |
| Craven, England | 1250–1500 | 40 |
| Peak District, England | 800–1200 | 75–83 |
| R. Mellte, Wales | 1600 | 16 |
| Mendip, England | 900–1100 | 40 |
| Slovenia, Yugoslavia | 1250–2000 | 10–100 |
| *Dry climates* | | |
| S. Algeria | 60 | 6 |
| Los Alamos, New Mexico, USA | 25–40 | < 1 |
| Grand Canyon, Colorado, USA | 25–40 | 7 |
| *Wet tropical climates* | | |
| R. Kissimee, Florida, USA | 1200 | 5 |
| Yucatan, Mexico | 1000–1500 | 12–44 |
| Indonesia | 200–3000 | 83 |

The Corbel erosion rate formula is:

$$X = \frac{ET_c}{10^d}$$

where E is the effective run-off and is the annual rainfall less evapotranspiration expressed in decimetres, $T_c$ is the calcium content in mg/l $CaCO_3$, d is the density of the limestone in $g/cm^3$, and X is the annual quantity of limestone removed in cubic metres per square kilometre per year ($m^3/km^2/yr$).

If the density is assumed to be 2.5 $g/cm^2$ the formula becomes:

$$X = \frac{4ET_c}{100}$$

For the Cheddar catchment in the Mendip Hills $T_c$ is 220 mg/l (see figure 77), the precipitation is 10.3 decimetres per year and the evapotranspiration 5.85 decimetres per year. Thus:

$$X = \frac{4\,(10.3 - 5.85)\,220}{100}$$

which is 39.2 $m^3/km^2/yr$.

Table 26 gives an indication of how limestone erosion rates vary on a world-wide scale.

It has been assumed throughout that limestone is almost solely composed of calcium carbonate. Some limestone, however, contains significant proportions of magnesium carbonate. Fortunately the method of analysis for magnesium in water is similar to that for calcium and where magnesium is present the Corbel equation can be modified to:

$$X = \frac{4E(T_c + T_m)}{100}$$

where $T_m$ is the concentration of magnesium expressed in mg/l $MgCO_3$.

For the Cheddar example the value for $T_m$ is 6 mg/l $MgCO_3$. The sum of calcium plus magnesium hardness values ($T_c + T_m$) is sometimes referred to as total water hardness and can also be measured using the BDH water hardness packs mentioned above.

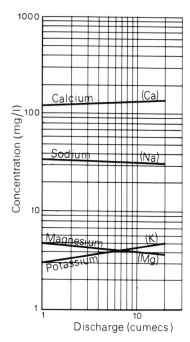

Discharge (cumecs)

*Variations in concentration for other solutions*
The variation of calcium in natural waters in limestone areas has
been studied in detail but less information can be obtained for the
concentration and variation of other common **ions** (the separate
electrically charged particles that many chemicals split into when
taken into solution in water). Some of these appear to follow a
similar pattern to that described for calcium in streams in that the
concentration decreases with increasing discharge; for other ions the
opposite situation occurs. There is also evidence that the pattern for
any individual ion will vary from river to river. The relationship
between discharge and ion concentration for differing elements is
shown in figure 80. These results are for the River Wensum in the
Norwich region. Some ions decrease in concentrations with increasing discharge (e.g. sodium and magnesium) while others show the
opposite relationship (e.g. calcium and potassium).

## The relationship of suspended to solute load

A graph of solute and suspended sediment concentrations for the
River Avon at Melksham is given in figure 77. The pattern of load
figures can be illustrated for the solute and suspended sediment concentrations that correspond to discharges of 4, 20, 50 and 100
cumecs. These values are obtained by using the 'best fit' lines given
in figure 77, and the appropriate concentration values are given in
table 27a.

   To convert the concentration figures to load multiply the concentration by the discharge. A concentration of 4 mg/l at a discharge
of 4 cumecs is a load value of 16 g (there are 1000 litres in a cumec).
The concentration values in table 27a are presented as load values in
table 27b. Figure 81 is a plot of the solute and concentration loads.
It is an instructive exercise to plot the combined solute and suspended loads on the same graph.

   The significance of the load graph in figure 81 is considerable. As
we saw above, the River Avon is carrying over six thousand times
more suspended sediment at 100 cumecs than at 4 cumecs. It is also
clear that the relative contributions of solute and suspended load are
very different at high and low discharges. There are two important
questions to ask. First, what is the relative frequency of high to low
discharge conditions, and second, how important is the very rare
flood which may occur only once in every 100 years?

   For the River Avon the graphs for suspended sediment and solute
load combined with flow frequency data show that 50% of the total
annual suspended sediment load is moved by flows that only occur
for 2% of the time; for solutes, 50% of the solute load is moved by
flows that occur for 20% of the time. Thus 50% of the suspended
sediment load, in an average year, is moved during a period of about
8 days.

   The answer to the second question is much less clear but many
geomorphologists would suggest that the rare, almost catastrophic,
event plays a very important role in both the removal of material
and in actual erosion. It is a case of comparing the slow and steady
every day event against the rare and capricious!

   Considerations of the material carried as stream load illustrate the
close relationship between hydrology and geomorphology. Except in
arid regions virtually all the weathering products are carried out of

Table 27   *Suspended sediment and solute for R. Avon, Melksham, Wiltshire*

| Discharge | 4 cumecs | 20 cumecs | 50 cumecs | 100 cumecs |
|---|---|---|---|---|
| *a. Concentrations (in mg/l)* | | | | |
| Suspended sediment concentration | 4 | 60 | 300 | 1 000 |
| Solute concentration | 500 | 310 | 240 | 200 |
| Total concentration | 504 | 370 | 540 | 1 200 |
| *b. Loads (in g/sec)* | | | | |
| Suspended sediment load | 16 | 1 200 | 15 000 | 100 000 |
| Solute load | 2 000 | 6 200 | 12 000 | 20 000 |
| Total load | 2 016 | 7 400 | 27 000 | 120 000 |

**81** Relationship of suspended sediment and solute load to discharge, R. Avon, Melksham, Wiltshire

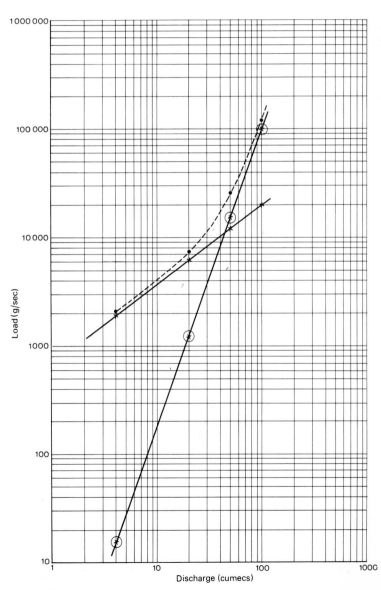

Load (g/sec)

Discharge (cumecs)

ⓧ  Suspended load
x   Solute load
●   Suspended and solute load

the catchment by fluvial transport. Similar transport must also occur on valley slopes, the material in that case being carried by the soil water. The velocity will be very much slower on the slopes and very little is known about the rate of erosion and transport in such sites. This is a topic awaiting further study by hydrologists and geomorphologists.

## Selected references

Rendle, P., Vokins, M. and Davis, P. 1972. *Experimental Chemistry: a Laboratory Manual.* 2nd edn. London: Arnold.

# 9

# River channel pattern

Whereas the term **drainage pattern** (see chapter 5) refers to the arrangement of channel links within a drainage network, by **channel pattern** we mean the shape of an individual channel as seen from above. Figures 82 to 84 show a number of channels and it is immediately apparent that river channels are rarely straight for any great length. Indeed straightness is often the result of disturbance of the flow by an obstruction or of local geological structures such as when a river follows major joints or fault-planes. Alternatively, such a channel may have been artificially straightened by man.

## Patterns

Three pattern forms that are generally identified are **braided**, when a channel divides into several parts (figure 82), **meandering**, when the channel twists (figure 83), and **straight**.

In a river we may find reaches of each of the three types at various points along its channel, and in practice it may be difficult at times to separate one pattern from another. A meandering river may not curve all along its length and there are likely to be straight and possibly even braided reaches, so we must recognise that whilst a channel may be described as of a particular pattern there may be reaches along it which do not strictly belong to the particular category. In practice a reach is not generally described as straight unless it is at least ten times longer than the width of the channel along that reach, and a river may be said to be essentially straight if the distance along its channel is no more than 1.1 times as great as that of a straight line from the start to finish of its channel.

A river is said to meander if the distance from a point A along its channel to a point B further down the channel is more than, or equal to, 1.5 times the distance from A to B measured along the valley. Thus in figure 84 the channel of the River Eden covers a distance of 10.8 km along a valley length of 7.2 km. The channel distance is 10.8/7.2 times greater than the valley length, i.e. 1.5 times greater, so it is an example of a meandering river.

It is likely that this value for the River Eden is a minimum value since it is difficult to measure very small deviations from course which could amount in practice to a significant total addition to channel length. For this reason measurements made by laying a piece of string along the mapped river course are probably as accurate as using a map measure. Also the river channel would tend to have minor irregularities of its course straightened during survey and upon reduction to scale. The ratio of channel distance to valley distance, known as the **sinuosity ratio**, measured from a map is thus likely to be less than it would be from a specific field measurement.

A compass survey in the field was made of the Llanddowror Stream, Dyfed, Wales, and the resulting map is shown in figure 85. A sinuosity ratio of 1.5 obtained from field measurements (450 paces:298 paces) may be compared with one of 1.48 from the Ordnance Survey map, thereby illustrating the slightly different readings likely to be obtained on the same stretch of river in the field and from a scaled down map. In this particular instance the difference may be critical for classification purposes — field measurement labels this stretch of river as meandering but map measurement does not. This example also illustrates the artificiality of having one particular value to demarcate between one form and another when river patterns present a continuum of forms from straight (sinuosity of 1.0) to extremely intricate meandering (sinuosity of up to 4.0).

One final word of caution may be added concerning the interpretation of sinuosity in natural channels. Close study of the Ordnance Survey maps may reveal that where meanders have been cut off naturally and are now marshy channels, the river itself has been artificially embanked, thereby retaining the straight channel that results after meander cut-off and inhibiting further meander development. Although the channel may have been cut naturally, the channel pattern is not in this case one the river would assume without man's intervention.

**84** Finding the sinuosity ratio for R. Eden, Cumbria

**85** *Below, left.* Plan of part of the course of Llanddowror Stream, Dyfed, Wales, made by compass traverse in the field. Measurement of distance was made by pacing

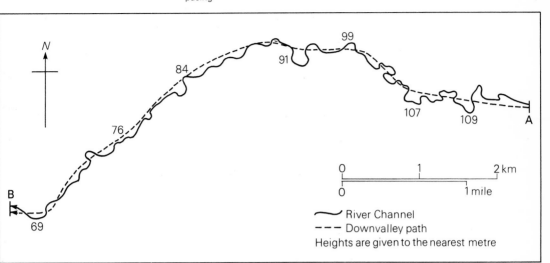

N

99

84

91

76

107

109

A

B

69

0       1       2 km

0             1 mile

~ River Channel
- - - Downvalley path
Heights are given to the nearest metre

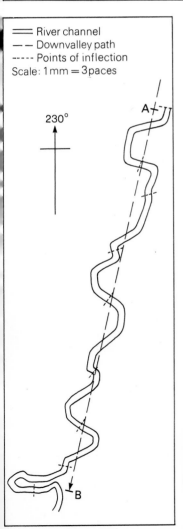

═══ River channel
— — Downvalley path
----- Points of inflection
Scale: 1 mm = 3 paces

230°

A

B

Bearing in mind the cautions given regarding measurement of the sinuosity ratio from a map, this ratio of channel distance to valley distance is nevertheless a useful measurement for making classifications of river channel more precise. We have said that three pattern forms are usually recognised, braided, meandering and straight. However, it has been observed from measurements of sinuosity ratios, both from maps and in the field, that for many channels the sinuosity ratio falls between 1.0 (straight) and 1.5 (meandering). We could either add a fourth category for patterns between these two values or use the term **sinuous** to apply to all channels with a sinuosity greater than 1.0.

## Straight channels

Laboratory studies of water flow through channels scaled down and created artificially in sand tanks or flumes cannot reproduce real situations exactly. Although channel size, water discharge and quantity of load can be controlled to a great extent, it is not possible to scale down load size or bed and bank materials and retain the same properties. Clay particles, which in a flume would be equivalent to sands in a natural river bed, are more cohesive, as explained in chapter 8, than the sands they represent. Usually very fine sand is used in such studies. In any case the scaling down cannot be possible if water is the liquid used for flow, as it usually is.

Despite such imperfections, flumes are useful since discharge, channel shape, load amounts and channel gradient are all easily controlled.

Studies of changes that take place when water is run through straight channels in laboratory flumes reveal that for a time the channel remains straight but changes take place in its width and in the distribution of sediment along its bed. Scouring and deposition produce shallows and deeps alternating along the bed, as illustrated in figure 86. The shallower channel sections are recognisable by ruffled water, while the deeps are comparatively quiet. Equivalent features in natural rivers have long been recognised by fishermen and in the USA the anglers' terms for them — **riffle** for a shallow and

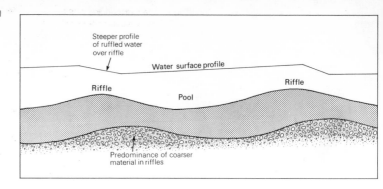

**86** Diagrammatic representation of a pool and riffle sequence

Table 28 *Measurements of depth of river channel in a reach of the Brook made at intervals across the channel along lines spaced at metre intervals upstream, as shown in figure 87*

| Distance along stream (metres) | Depth of stream in cm at each point – reading in order from the left bank | | | | | | | | | | | |
|---|---|---|---|---|---|---|---|---|---|---|---|---|
| | left bank 1 | 2 | 3 | 4 | 5 | 6 | 7 | 8 | 9 | 10 | 11 | 12 |
| 0 | 2.5 | 4 | 4 | 2 | 2 | 3.5 | 4 | – | – | – | – | – | – |
| 1 | 0.5 | 3.5 | 5 | 3.5 | 3.5 | 6.0 | 5.5 | – | – | – | – | – | – |
| 2 | 1 | 2.5 | 2.5 | 5.5 | 4.0 | – | – | – | – | – | – | – | – |
| 3 | 0 | 2.0 | 5.0 | 3.5 | 5.0 | 2.5 | – | – | – | – | – | – | – |
| 4 | 1 | 2.0 | 3.0 | 3.0 | 2.5 | 5.5 | – | – | – | – | – | – | – |
| 5 | 1 | 2.0 | 2.0 | 0.5 | 4.0 | 3.0 | 3.0 | – | – | – | – | – | – |
| 6 | 0 | 1 | 1.5 | 2.5 | 0.5 | 0.5 | 3.5 | 5.0 | – | – | – | – | – |
| 7 | 3.5 | 2.5 | 2.5 | 2.0 | 1.0 | 1.5 | 0.5 | 2.5 | 4.0 | 4.0 | – | – | – |
| 8 | 0 | 2.0 | 0.5 | 1.0 | 2.5 | 4.0 | 4.0 | 2.0 | 2.0 | 1.5 | 2.5 | 3.0 | |
| 9 | +1.0 | +1.0 | +1.0 | 0 | +1.0 | 3.5 | 4.0 | 5.0 | 4.0 | 4.5 | 5.0 | 1.0 | |
| 10 | 1.0 | +3.0 | 1.0 | 5.0 | 3.5 | 5.0 | 4.0 | 4.0 | +0.5 | – | – | – | |
| 11 | 3.0 | 3.5 | 5.5 | 7.0 | 4.0 | 4.5 | 0.5 | 0 | – | – | – | – | |
| 12 | 0 | 2.5 | 4.5 | 5.5 | 5.0 | 2.5 | 1.5 | 0.5 | – | – | – | – | |
| 13 | 2.0 | 7.0 | 6.0 | 3.0 | 1.5 | 4.0 | 4.5 | 1.5 | 2.0 | 0.5 | – | – | |
| 14 | 2.5 | 3.5 | 3.5 | 2.0 | 3.0 | 6.0 | 1.0 | 1.0 | +2.0 | +3.0 | – | – | |
| 15 | 0 | 1.0 | 4.0 | 4.0 | 5.0 | 6.0 | 3.0 | 3.5 | 4.0 | 0.5 | 0 | – | |
| 16 | 0 | 0 | +1.0 | 1.0 | 3.0 | 4.5 | 4.0 | 5.5 | 0 | 2.5 | 2 | – | |
| 17 | 0 | 1.0 | 2.0 | 4.0 | 5.0 | 8.0 | 9.0 | 4.0 | 0.5 | – | – | – | |
| 18 | +1.5 | +1.5 | +1.5 | 0 | 1.5 | 5.0 | 3.0 | 4.0 | 4.0 | 3.0 | – | – | |
| 19 | +4.0 | +4.0 | +4.0 | +3.0 | 4.0 | 7.0 | 8.0 | 5.0 | 7.5 | – | – | – | |

Positive signs indicate points where ground rises above water level

Table 29 *Bed load size along the Brook, Dyfed, Wales, from samples of 25 particles taken from a circle of approximately 7 cm radius at each location shown in figure 87*

| Location | Number of particles falling into each size class (b-axis) | | | | | | | | | | | | |
|---|---|---|---|---|---|---|---|---|---|---|---|---|---|
| | Width of particles in mm | | | | | | | | | | | | |
| | 1–5 | 6–10 | 11–15 | 16–20 | 21–25 | 26–30 | 31–35 | 36–40 | 41–45 | 46–50 | 51–55 | 56–60 | 61+ |
| 1. Riffle | 0 | 0 | 0 | 5 | 3 | 5 | 2 | 3 | 2 | 2 | 1 | 0 | 2 |
| 2. Pool | 1 | 2 | 4 | 8 | 3 | 1 | 1 | 1 | 1 | 0 | 1 | 0 | 1 |
| 3. Riffle | 0 | 0 | 5 | 5 | 10 | 2 | 0 | 0 | 0 | 1 | 0 | 1 | 1 |
| 4. Pool | 0 | 11 | 4 | 4 | 1 | 1 | 0 | 2 | 0 | 0 | 1 | 0 | 1 |
| 5. Riffle | 0 | 2 | 3 | 6 | 5 | 4 | 2 | 2 | 0 | 0 | 0 | 1 | 0 |
| 6. Pool | 0 | 3 | 8 | 5 | 2 | 4 | 1 | 1 | 0 | 0 | 0 | 1 | 0 |

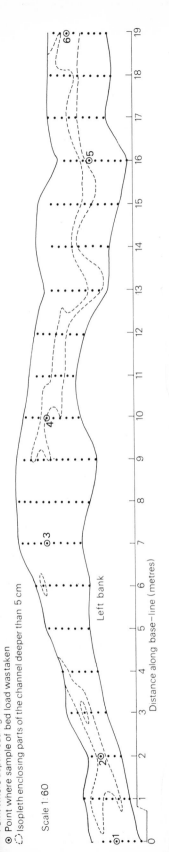

Scale 1:60

Left bank

Distance along base–line (metres)

**87** *Left.* Plan of a straight reach of the Brook, Dyfed, Wales, with points plotted for locating depth measurements given in table 28

**88** Bed load size along the Brook, Dyfed, Wales. Histogram of the first two samples of table 29

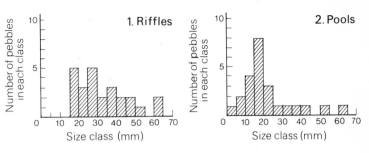

pool for a deep — have now passed into general use.

A study made of a relatively straight reach of the Brook, near Pendine, Dyfed, Wales, is tabulated in table 28 and a plan of the reach is shown in figure 87. Plotting depths of the channel on the plan and drawing isopleths (i.e. lines of equal depth, at intervals of 10 mm) will reveal a succession of such pools and riffles.

Table 29 gives the results of the measurement of widths (i.e. measurements along the short or b-axes) of samples of the twenty-five largest particles on the stream bed, both on riffles and in pools. The exact location of each sample is shown in figure 87. Figure 88 shows the measurements for samples one and two, taken on a riffle and in a pool respectively and plotted as histograms. Comparison of the two histograms reveals that particles are coarser on the riffle than in the pool. Such a sample is of course too small and requires corroboration. This may be obtained if the remaining sample measurements are plotted similarly.

An explanation *why* a riffle and pool sequence is produced remains to be found; it seems to be in the nature of water flow within a channel. The observation of the relationship between coarser particle sizes and riffles enables us to surmise *how* the riffle and pool sequence is formed.

Pools and riffles are, as a rule, only present in channels with bed material coarser than sand, and develop in particular when a river's load comprises particles of many different sizes. Generally, of course, the two characteristics will be found together, as streams with a bed load this coarse are rarely homogeneous in grade. One characteristic of deposits of mixed sizes is that when they are shaken about the coarser particles tend to rise and lie upon the surface of river bed deposits where they are moved along. It has already been shown in chapter 8 (figure 72) that the size of particle moved depends upon stream velocity. Since velocity is rarely constant a particle will generally move in a series of jerks. As a particle comes to rest, particularly if it is large in relation to the water's depth, there will be increased turbulence around it, reducing water velocity. As other particles approach it they enter water travelling at slightly lower velocity, and it may be that this causes a group of coarse particles to build up. This, in turn, creates a steeper channel profile at the down-stream end, as illustrated in figure 89. As the profile increases so velocity also increases until it at last overcomes the effect of increased turbulence and allows particles to proceed upon their way. This takes place over the bed below the riffle, in the comparatively deeper pool (figure 87). The particle continues until once again it comes to rest at a point which becomes a riffle. Measurements made of the water surface and river bed profiles at low water on the

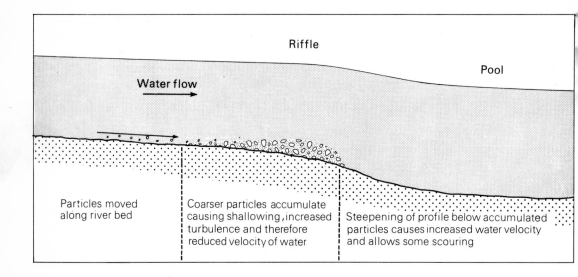

Middle River, Virginia, USA (figure 94a) show the manner in which the water profile shallows significantly at a riffle and steepens on its lower side, indicating the increased gradient required to maintain sufficient velocity to overcome turbulence and support its load at these points. A bed profile can be drawn for the path of deepest water along the channel of the Brook — this shows the shallowing associated with riffles along even the fastest flowing path in the channel.

The account given above may explain the manner in which riffles grow in straight river sections but, as has been pointed out, it does not give the reason for their formation. Riffles tend to be fairly stable, re-forming in similar positions after the subsidence of high discharges which may move the whole bed along. This fact needs explanation, as does the comparatively regular spacing of the riffle and pool sequence.

Comparison between the distance from the lower end of the first riffle to the next and the width of the channel for the Brook (figure 87) gives a ratio of 7.25:1. Between the beginnings of the second and third riffle there is a distance of 10.25 m, but here the channel is wider (1.5 m) so the ratio becomes 10.25:1.5, or 6.8, a very similar value. Table 30 gives further lengths between riffles together with the channel widths for a longer section of the Brook. Calculation of the ratios will show only a small variation. Large numbers of measurements on channels of different sizes show a similar range of figures for the spacing of the riffle and pool sequence, most values lying between five and seven times the channel width.

It is widely recognised that the width (w) of a river is closely related to the mean annual discharge ($\overline{Q}$). This relationship may be expressed as $W = k.\ \overline{Q}$, where k is a constant which varies from river to river, and from point to point along any particular river, and has to be found empirically for each point.

Width being the common factor, this relationship therefore indicates a relationship between riffle and pool spacing and discharge, and so an understanding of the nature of flow of water itself would help with the understanding of riffle spacing.

Table 30 *Pool and riffle measurements and channel width along the Brook, Dyfed, Wales*

| Pool Length (m) | Riffle length (m) | Combined lengths | Width (m) | Ratio |
|---|---|---|---|---|
| 3.5 | 4.25 | 7.75 | 1.0 | 7.75 |
| 5.0 | 5.25 | 10.25 | 1.5 | 6.8 |
| 5.8 | 3.2 | 9.0 | 1.5 | |
| 4.6 | 3.3 | 7.9 | 1.8 | |
| 7.0 | 3.1 | 10.1 | 1.5 | |
| 4.0 | 2.1 | 6.1 | 1.5 | |
| 4.0 | 3.0 | 7.0 | 1.5 | |
| 3.6 | 2.4 | 6.0 | 1.5 | |
| 4.9 | 2.5 | 7.4 | 1.0 | |

Observation of the path of the deepest part of the channel of the Brook (figure 87) reveals that, even in this comparatively straight reach of the stream, the fastest (deepest) water threads a sinuous course. This is in fact a characteristic of straight channels. It would appear to be a natural propensity of water to flow in a sinuous course. Even meltwater with little or no load flowing across ice, a medium presenting little friction to flow, assumes a meandering course.

If the sinuosity of a stream arises like pool and riffle spacing from the nature of channelled flow itself, one might expect a relationship to exist between the sinuosity of a stream and its discharge similar to that between riffle and pool spacing and discharge.

## Sinuosity

Research work has concentrated upon channel patterns classified as meandering. It is clearly easier to measure sinuous patterns in a distinctly meandering river and we, too, shall use clear features of this kind to illustrate the following section. However, if the relationships found for riffle spacing in straight channels are also found to be true of meandering ones, we would expect the same general tendencies to be true of channels with degrees of sinuosity between 1 and 1.5.

The problems of identifying meander shape measurements, or parameters, may be seen if figure 90 which defines these parameters

**90** Parameters of meandering streams

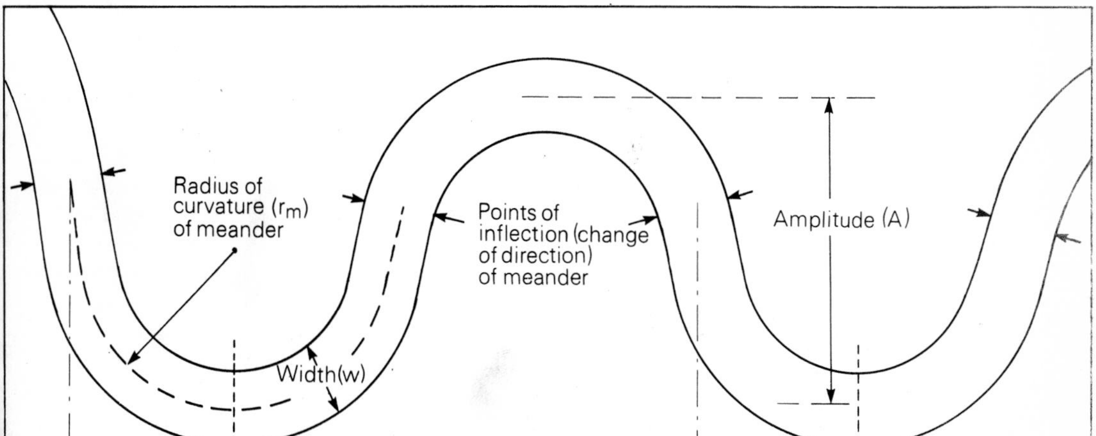

Radius of curvature ($r_m$) of meander
Points of inflection (change of direction) of meander
Amplitude (A)
Width(w)
Wavelength (λ)
Axis of meander

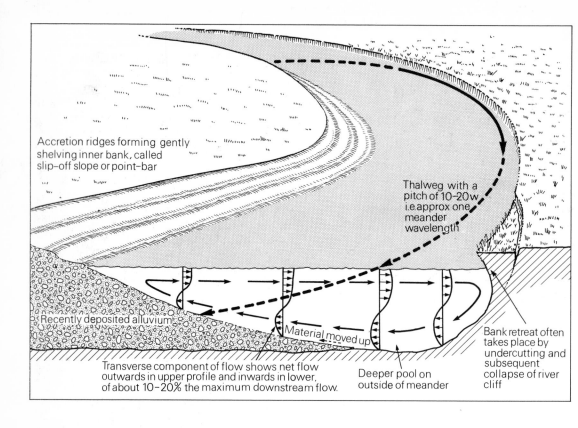

Accretion ridges forming gently
shelving inner bank, called
slip–off slope or point–bar

Thalweg with a
pitch of 10–20 w
i.e. approx one
meander
wavelength

Recently deposited alluvium

Material moved up

Bank retreat often
takes place by
undercutting and
subsequent
collapse of river
cliff

Transverse component of flow shows net flow
outwards in upper profile and inwards in lower,
of about 10–20% the maximum downstream flow.

Deeper pool on
outside of meander

and, for example, figure 84 are compared. Clearly the measurements
would be difficult to make for many sinuous channels. The location
of points of inflection for measuring wavelength ($\lambda$) of meanders, for
instance, is often an arbitrary decision. The distance between successive axes of similar bends may often be taken instead, as in the
example given in figure 95, but once again the location of a bend
axis is not easy to state.

One feature of the river channel which can be identified fairly
clearly, by measuring the depths across the channel at regular distances along it, is the **thalweg**, the thread of fastest flowing water.
Following the course of the thalweg around a meander it is seen to
swing to the outside of each bend at a point just below the axis of
the bend, as illustrated in figure 91. It is easy to see that where this
faster water impinges on the channel side some undercutting of the
bank may take place, wearing the bank away. Material eroded from
the bank is carried along in the stream.

Suspended particles and bed load fragments, which are moved
along by the thalweg current in particular, may be carried laterally
by small eddies which leave the faster current to enter slacker flow,
over a shoal for example, where some deposition is likely to occur as
velocities fall. Erosion of a bank where the thalweg impinges may
therefore be compensated by growth of deposits in shoals (**point-
bars**) of slacker water further downstream. Such shoals develop
particularly opposite points where the thalweg strikes one bank,
leaving a broad stretch of shallower, more turbulent and therefore
slacker water against the other. Thus, as one bank retreats by erosion,

**92** Very tightly developed meanders on the River Forth, looking eastwards (downstream from Stirling, NS790940), cut into glacial outwash materials and alluvium. Note the narrow neck of the meander in the left middle distance. The Ochil Hills lie beyond

**93** Looking downstream along the River Severn (SJ615046) towards Ironbridge Gorge, the nearest meanders clearly show erosion of the outer banks, deposition on the inner, and close study will reveal bowed depositional ridges across the inner cores of the meanders, showing their patterns of growth

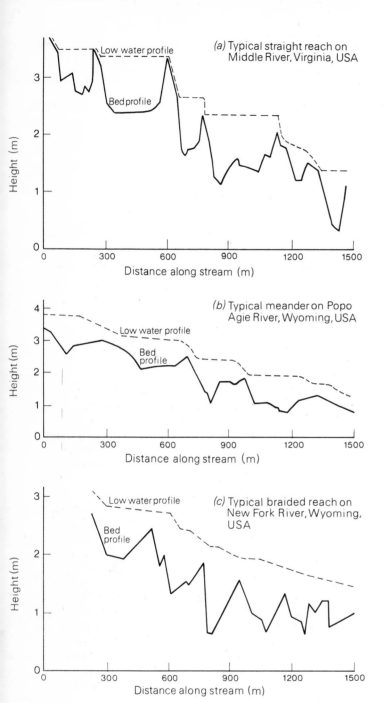

**94** Profiles of three rivers including straight, meandering and braided reaches

(a) Typical straight reach on Middle River, Virginia, USA

(b) Typical meander on Popo Agie River, Wyoming, USA

(c) Typical braided reach on New Fork River, Wyoming, USA

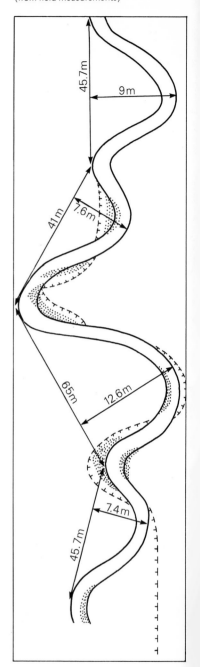

**95** Plan of the channel of an unnamed tributary of R. Aire, Yorkshire, showing wavelength and amplitude of meander (from field measurements)

Table 31   *Pool and riffle measurements and channel width along an unnamed tributary of R. Aire*

| Pool length (m) | Riffle length (m) | Combined lengths | Width (m) | Ratio |
|---|---|---|---|---|
| 8.4 | 12.2 | 20.6 | 2.7 | 7.6 |
| 15.2 | 6.9 | 22.1 | 3.8 | 5.8 |
| 3.8 | 10.7 | 14.5 | 4.0 | 3.8 |
| 6.9 | 3.8 | 10.7 | 4.3 | 2.5 |
| 9.0 | 12.2 | 21.2 | 3.5 | 6.0 |
| 12.95 | 11.43 | 24.4 | 4.5 | 5.4 |
| 9.2 | 5.4 | 14.6 | 2.6 | 5.6 |
| 6.9 | 20.6 | 27.5 | 2.6 | 10.6 |
| 9.9 | 9.9 | 19.8 | 2.5 | 7.9 |
| 16.0 | 15.2 | 31.2 | 3.7 | 8.4 |
| 13.0 | 3.1 | 16.1 | 2.4 | 6.7 |
| 14.5 | 6.9 | 21.4 | 3.1 | 6.9 |
| 11.4 | 2.3 | 13.7 | 2.1 | 6.5 |
| | | | Mean ratio = | 6.4 |

the other advances by deposition, and a meander will tend to grow (figure 91). Since the energy required for erosion to take place arises through the downstream momentum of water flow, erosion carves the bank back and in a downstream direction as well, as illustrated in figure 97a and also in figure 92.

Meander growth, as described so far, is dependent, in part at least, upon the nature of the bank material. Easily eroded banks alongside the river obviously help meander development by allowing growth and by contributing material for deposition further downstream as point-bars. Well-formed meanders are, therefore, generally associated with stretches where the channel is cut through alluvium or similar deposits, such as clays or consolidated gravels (figure 93). Where banks are cut into more resistant rocks meander development will be restricted and the resulting sinuosity of the channel may temporarily be less. However, well-formed meanders are certainly found cut into solid rock channels, a classic area in Britain being in the Wye Valley at Symonds Yat, Herefordshire. The tendency towards meandering appears to prevail in all river channels, and at all points along a river channel.

Tracing the thalweg depth and water surface profile in a meandering channel produces a similar result (figure 94b) to that which we have seen in a straight channel (figure 94a). Pool-like features are associated with the outward swing near the axis of the bend whilst shallows or riffles are found at the points of inflection of a meander. Thus for each complete meander as defined in figure 90 there are two successive riffles and pools. Therefore if there is any connection between riffle formation and meanders the length of the channel in a meander should be about twice the distance between riffles in straight channels. We found the latter to be between five and seven times the width of the channel.

Along the meandering channel of an unnamed tributary of the River Aire, Yorkshire, England, measurements have been made of the spacing of pools and riffles (table 31) which, together with the associated channel widths, give figure 95. It can be seen that the results do lie close to the values found for straight channels. Table 32 gives further measurements made on the River Aire itself which

Table 32  *Pool and riffle measurements and channel width along R. Aire*

| Pool length (m) | Riffle length (m) | Width (m) |
|---|---|---|
| 14.5 | 25.9 | 9.3 |
| 34.3 | 13.0 | 9.4 |
| 20.6 | 15.2 | 9.6 |
| 28.7 | 22.1 | 9.8 |
| 22.1 | 14.5 | 9.57 |
| 46.5 | 24.4 | 9.6 |
| 26.7 | 20.6 | 9.6 |
| 14.5 | 35.0 | 9.5 |
| 11.4 | 35.8 | 9.4 |
| 40.3 | 16.8 | 9.3 |
| 18.3 | 38.9 | 9.2 |
| 37.3 | 22.1 | 9.2 |
| 28.9 | 23.7 | 9.3 |
| 18.4 | 34.5 | 9.3 |
| 32.8 | 14.5 | 9.4 |
| 8.38 | 22.1 | 9.4 |
| 41.9 | 16.8 | 9.4 |
| 21.3 | 25.1 | 9.2 |
| 10.7 | 14.5 | 9.0 |
| 31.1 | 42.7 | 9.3 |

Table 33  *Riffle spacing and channel width along Loughton Brook, Epping Forest (from field measurements)*

| Riffle spacing (m) | Channel width (m) | Riffle spacing (m) | Channel width (m) |
|---|---|---|---|
| 15 | 2 | 12 | 2 |
| 11 | 2 | 16 | 2 |
| 21 | 3 | 15 | 2 |
| 22 | 3 | 7 | 2 |
| 4 | 2 | 6 | 2 |
| 18 | 2 | 10 | 2 |
| 22 | 3 | 24 | 3 |
| 12 | 2 | 15 | 3 |
| 14 | 2 | 15 | 3 |
| 14 | 2 | 10 | 3 |
| 17 | 3 | 28 | 3 |
| 19 | 3 | 17 | 3 |
| 28 | 3 | 17 | 3 |
| 11 | 2 | 28 | 3 |
| 12 | 2 | 15 | 3 |
| 9 | 2 | 30 | 3 |
| 10 | 2 | 7 | 3 |
| 13 | 2 | 16 | 3 |
| 14 | 2 | 24 | 3 |
| 14 | 2 | | |

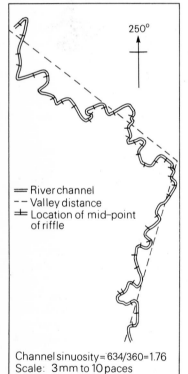

250°

— River channel
-- Valley distance
⊥ Location of mid-point of riffle

Channel sinuosity = 634/360 = 1.76
Scale: 3mm to 10 paces

**96** Plan of Loughton Brook, Epping Forest, showing channel sinuosity and the location of riffles along the river bed (from field measurements). Note the close coincidence of observed locations of riffles with points of inflection of meanders

may be used for further comparison, as can table 33, for Loughton Brook, Epping Forest, England and the plan in figure 96.

In figures 83 and 85, which show the channels of rather less sinuous streams, the difficulty of locating points of inflection is clearly apparent. Nevertheless, an attempt has been made and the locations are marked. Table 34 records the distances measured in the field between these points. The ratio of channel length to channel width for each complete meander lies generally between ten and fourteen. These values are twice those found for riffle and pool spacing in a straight channel and, since each complete meander contains two successive riffles and pools, confirm that a connection exists between riffles in straight channels and the formation of meanders.

The relationships shown above are often given in a more indirect way by comparing meander wavelength ($\lambda$) (see figure 90) with channel width. Numerous measurements of channels of many sizes indicate values for the wavelength ranging between seven and ten times the channel width ($w$). Measured along the channel itself, for a channel of sinuosity of 1.5, this gives values for the length of a complete meander between 10.5w and 15w, which is very close to those of 10w and 14w given above.

Thus we may generalise the relationship found for sinuous channels in the form $\lambda = a \times w$, where $a$ is a constant ranging approximately between 7 and 10.

Although the sinuosity of channels ranges between 1.0 and 4.0, the median value appears to approximate to 1.5. Using this value we can see that there are similar, although more approximate, relationships between the amplitude (A) and radius of curvature ($r_m$) of meanders (figure 90) and the channel width ($w$), which may be expressed generally as $A = b \times w$ and $r_m = c \times w$, where $b$ and $c$ are

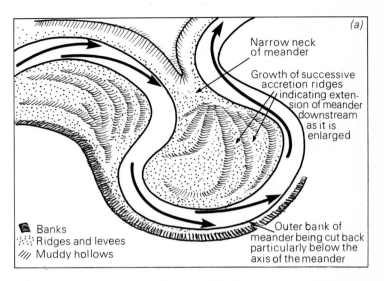

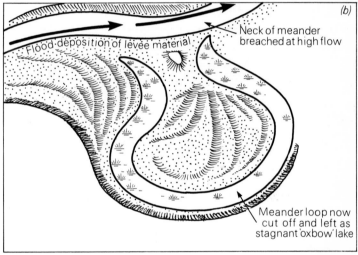

**Table 34** *Meander channel lengths between points of inflection and channel widths along part of Llanddowror Stream, Dyfed, Wales (from field measurements)*

| Distance along channel (m) between points of inflection | Channel width (m) | Ratio |
|---|---|---|
| 64.0 | 5.0 | 12.8 |
| 72.0 | 5.0 | 14.4 |
| 47.5 | 5.0 | 9.5 |
| 62.5 | 5.0 | 12.5 |
| 72.5 | 5.0 | 14.5 |
| 53.5 | 5.0 | 10.7 |
| 53.5 | 5.0 | 10.7 |
| 28.0 | 3.5 | 8.0 |
| 77.5 | 6.0 | 12.9 |
| | | Mean = 11.8 |

further constants. Amplitude, and therefore the constant b, varies quite considerably and appears to be particularly related to bank erodibility. The constant, c, for the relationship between radius of curvature and channel width, as measured for a large sample of different sized channels in the USA, was found to vary between 1.5 and 4.3 for two-thirds of the channels, with a median value around 2.7. Studies of pipe curvature have shown that a value of 2.0 gives minimum resistance due to curvature and it has been tentatively suggested that water flow in channels will tend to produce meanders on such a curvature. The exact form of resultant meanders, however, is to a large extent influenced by the bank materials and their erodibility.

Laboratory studies of meanders in flume channels suggest that channels cut in homogeneous materials do not increase in meander amplitude as bends progress downstream. However, rarely, if ever, is the material into which a channel is cut homogeneous. In any case discharge usually also increases downstream, and a general characteristic of meander development in alluvial materials in particular is

that channels *do* increase in meander amplitude downstream. As meander amplitude increases the neck of the meander decreases in width and may eventually be broken through completely (figure 97). If this happens, particularly during high river flow, deposition in the slack water of the former meander loop may in time plug the entrance to the loop and seal it off as an **oxbow lake**, which may eventually silt up to become a marshy hollow. Such abandoned loops are usually known as **cut-offs** (figure 98).

We saw in chapter 6 that the shape of a channel affects the efficiency of flow within it. If bank and bed material are quite resistant to erosion less material is provided for river load. In such streams the bed load may be in constant migration at almost all states of river flow, with the result that stream energy, after overcoming friction and transporting load, may act not only on the banks but on the bed of the stream as well. If the energy available is sufficient to erode, albeit slowly, it is possible that in channels cut in hard rock more downcutting may take place than channel widening. The channel form becomes relatively deep and narrow and consequently more efficient, so allowing even more energy for channel erosion. It should be noted, however, that although the presence of bed load over a channel floor may suggest that the stream is not deepening its bed at a particular time, it is most significant if the stream bed is still mantled with bed load material during bank-full or greater discharges when stream erosion must be considerably greater.

So far we have not considered the effects of gradient on channel pattern. Like channel shape and bank materials, this also affects a

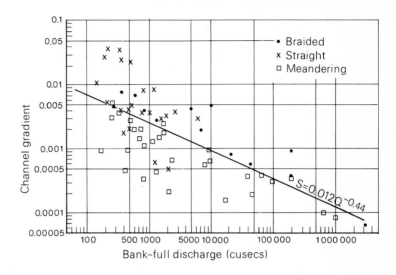

stream's energy. Figure 99 shows some relationships between channel pattern and stream gradient for rivers of all sizes. From this it would appear that straight channels bear no relation to channel gradient but are associated with small discharges. This suggests confirmation of the relationship between sinuosity and the ability of streams to erode their banks, in that streams with small discharges may be less able to erode their banks to any great extent.

### Braided patterns

A clear relationship, however, does appear to exist between channel gradient and channel pattern for streams which are not straight. Meandering streams have gradients less steep than braided streams; there is quite a sharp distinction shown in figure 99. It is apparent that immediately channel gradient exceeds a critical value compared with channel discharge ($S = 0.012Q^{-0.44}$), shown by the straight line, the channel changes from a meandering to a braided one.

Just as there is a gradual transition from straight streams through all grades of sinuosity so it is not easy at times to know whether a stream should be labelled braided or not. Braided streams are characterised by a number of channel segments which continuously part to flow around islands and rejoin further downstream (figures 82 and 100). Most streams have reaches containing alluvial islands sometimes so closely spaced as to be almost continuous, yet do not necessarily merit classification as braided. Generally there needs to be more than two channel segments in a reach before it is termed braided. The River Feshie (figure 82) is clearly braided in places, especially at medium discharges. Figure 100 shows a common condition of braiding today, that of a glacial outwash plain (or **sandur**). Conditions here suggest a relationship with heavily load-charged waters flowing in channels with very unstable banks, composed of incoherent sand and gravel with little vegetation to bind them. Similar conditions obviously occur in semi-arid regions of the world. The constant collapse of the bank does not permit the more characteristic single channel to form. Instead the channel widens and shallows. Deposited sand and pebbles on the channel floor may prove more resistant to

113

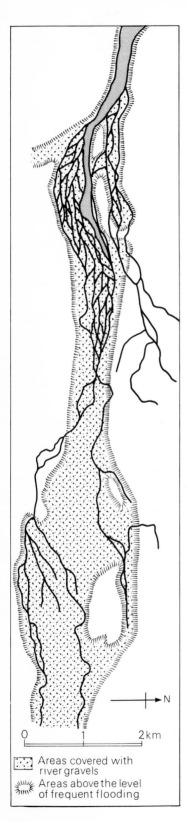

Areas covered with
river gravels

Areas above the level
of frequent flooding

further movement than the bank material, and may remain while the
latter is swept downstream. With their coarser bed loads, and
broader, shallower channels it follows (chapter 6) that braided
streams are characterised (figure 100) by steeper channel gradients
than their meandering counterparts, in order to maintain discharge.
Some observations have been made of braided channels which seem
consistent with the processes suggested above. Characteristically a
central bar grows in a manner similar to that of riffle growth, and
tends to concentrate flow into flanking channels which may be
enlarged if banks are not too resistant. Such enlargement of flanking
channels leads to a fall in the level of the water which may expose
the central bar as an island. Ultimately, if the island remains for long
enough, colonisation and stabilisation by plants may occur. Once the
channel splits around a bar or island, flow becomes less efficient than
if it were all in one channel and therefore requires steeper gradients.
In other respects, however, braided channels have similar characteristics to meandering. Figure 94c shows the similarity of thalweg
depth profiles, for example, in that there is a succession of shallows
and deeps, and steepening of the water surface profile occurs at the
downstream ends of the shallows.

The difference in gradient which separates meandering from
braided channel forms, separates in fact channels with stable and
unstable banks respectively. Indeed the line on figure 99 closely
corresponds to the gradient at which the minimum effort is needed
to move the river load. Collapse of unstable banks increases the river
load and the river may have to increase its gradient to acquire enough
power to move the load. The rivers plotted on figure 99 all have
channels cut into alluvium so the results specifically refer to such
alluvial channels. Channels cut into bedrock are unlikely to braid
owing to the stability of bank materials, but if the delineating
gradient is between stable and unstable channels it would seem likely
that instability of bedrock channels at gradients greater than this
characteristic angle would be apparent in some form, and seems to
be that meanders are three to four times longer than alluvial
meanders when cut into bedrock at these gradients.

Quantitative measurements in the field and laboratory are leading
to a closer understanding of the complex inter-relationships that
exist between channel discharge, sediment load, channel shape,
gradient and pattern. There is scope for a considerable variety of
interesting small scale but detailed studies of the kind indicated in
this chapter.

### Selected references

Leopold, L.B., Wolman, M.G., and Miller, J.P. 1964. *Fluvial Processes in
Geomorphology*. San Francisco: W.H. Freeman.
Morisawa, M. 1968. *Streams, Their Dynamics and Morphology*. New York:
McGraw-Hill.

# 10

# The importance of the drainage basin

The study and measurement of processes operating upon the landscape can be rewarding not only in their own academic right but also in terms of their useful technical application.

We have indicated in chapter 3 how calculations of soil moisture amounts are important, in conjunction with plant root constants, for indicating when and by how much to irrigate. Long term calculations from meteorological data and a knowledge of the soil moisture characteristics can be used to indicate drought frequencies by using the methods demonstrated with flood data in chapter 7. From this the cost of droughts in terms of loss of plant growth can be calculated and set against the cost of installing and using irrigation and decisions made about its practicability. With their growing use of technology and efforts to increase yields, even marginally, farmers are likely to be in need of such calculations in coming years.

Relationships between changing land use and its effect upon run-off were indicated in chapter 4 and upon river load in chapter 8. Considerable change occurs when building construction takes place on formerly cultivated land. During construction itself erosion is increased, causing sediment load to increase and possibly sedimentation problems further downstream. Evidence is being accumulated now that urbanisation causes more rapid run-off, contributing to both flooding and drought. Permeable land surface (see chapter 4) is partially replaced by impermeable roof tops and paved surfaces from which run-off is quickly channelled into pipes leading directly to rivers. A similar, though lesser, effect has probably been produced over centuries of development of subsoil field drainage. This latter rapid drainage now contributes to the growing amount of nitrates which are washed through soils after fertiliser applications and which are causing concern by their impairment of water quality. Legislation is increasing as more and more demand is placed upon rivers for water supplies and more and more effluent is put into them. Demand has risen as the rivers' tolerance of effluent has decreased.

There are numerous examples all over the world of the quite massive schemes for the transfer of freshwater supplies from one part of a country to another. From a local self-sufficiency we have moved into an era of a real interdependence which in turn has economic and political implications. In the British Isles the national perception has been that water is abundant. Supplying authorities were therefore charged with maintaining supplies almost regardless of cost and a flat-rate charge was made to domestic consumers regardless of the amount used. Even so, the introduction of more realistic economic charges in 1974 caused such concern that the national perception must have been challenged; and it was challenged again during the 1976 drought (see chapter 7). Calculations have shown that it would now be economic to meter domestic supplies in south-east England. Other countries have often had need to regard water supply and its use more highly, but there is no doubt that during the past decade or so quite massive interest has attached to hydrology, which merely reflects the growing understanding of the importance of water to us all.

# APPENDIX

# Using logarithmic paper

Any number can be expressed as a logarithm, and logarithm tables usually give the value to the base 10. That is to say that any number can be represented as 10 to the power of some value, let us say x. This is usually written $10^x$.

The logarithm of a number is the power value, x. So 100, which can be written as $10^2$, has the logarithm 2.0000. $10^1$ is 10, and $10^0$ is 1. $10^{-1}$ is 1/10, $10^{-2}$ is 1/100, and so on. Hence any value between, say, 10 and 100 can be represented by 10 to the power of 'one-point-something' and we use logarithm tables to find what that 'something' value is.

The usefulness of logarithms for multiplication or division is that one simply needs to add or subtract the logarithm, which is usually easier than multiplying or dividing the original numbers. It follows that if a series of numbers increases by regular multiples, such as 2, 4, 8, 16, 32, 64, etc. their logarithms increase simply by adding the same amount each time. The logarithm of 4 is 0.6021. Adding 0.3010 (the logarithm of 2) gives 0.9031 which is the logarithm of 8. Adding 0.3010 again gives the logarithm of 16.

If a series of numbers rise by regular additions they appear as a straight line on ordinary graph paper, but if they rise by regular multiples, they produce a curve. In geography many features increase or decrease by regular multiples, geometrically, rather than by additions. Examples are the number of streams plotted against their order (figure 43), size of basins against order (figure 48) and stream lengths plotted against order (figure 45). Plotted on ordinary graph paper the power relationship would be difficult to see. Plotting the logarithms of the values would produce a

straight line and indicate that there is a 'power relationship'. To save looking up the logarithm of each value, specially drawn logarithmic graph paper may be used instead and the arithmetic values plotted direct, as in figures 43, 45 and 48.

Semi-logarithmic graph paper (figure 101) has one axis divided logarithmically whilst the other axis has ordinary, arithmetic, divisions. The logarithmic axis is divided into 'cycles', each cycle being numbered from 1 to 9. Any number of cycles may be used. That shown here has three cycles which means that it can represent numbers over three power cycles. It could be from 1 to 10 in the first cycle, 10 to 100 in the second and 100 to 1000 in the third. Alternatively, the cycles may represent from 0.1 to 100, from 0.01 to 10, from 10 to 10 000, and so on, according to the values which need plotting.

When using logarithmic graph paper the first thing to do is to find the range of values needed, to select the appropriate number of cycles and to number the axis. Figures 43 and 45 show two cycles being used but numbered differently. Figure 47 uses one cycle whilst figure 48 uses three and figure 49 uses seven. Having chosen and labelled the cycles accordingly, the values can be plotted as on ordinary, arithmetic, graph paper, but care should be taken as the spaces do not always represent the same values. In figure 101 the lines from 1 to 5 represent divisions of 0.1; from 5 to 10 they represent divisions of 0.2.

The value of logarithmic paper, then, is that power relationships are shown as straight lines so that the relationship is clear, and since it is easier to draw straight lines than curves, intermediate values can be

read off with some degree of confidence. It is also useful, of course, when one wishes to plot a large range of values, especially when there is a large number of values at the lower end of the scale, so it is also used for instance when plotting settlement sizes.

Figure 102 shows graph paper on which both axes are divided logarithmically. This is known as 'Log.-log.' graph paper and it is used in the same way as semi-logarithmic paper. Figures 9, 73 and 81 illustrate various types of this paper.

### Selected references

Schemel, I. July 1977. The usefulness of logarithmic graphs. *Teaching Geography*. Geographical Association, pp. 19–21.

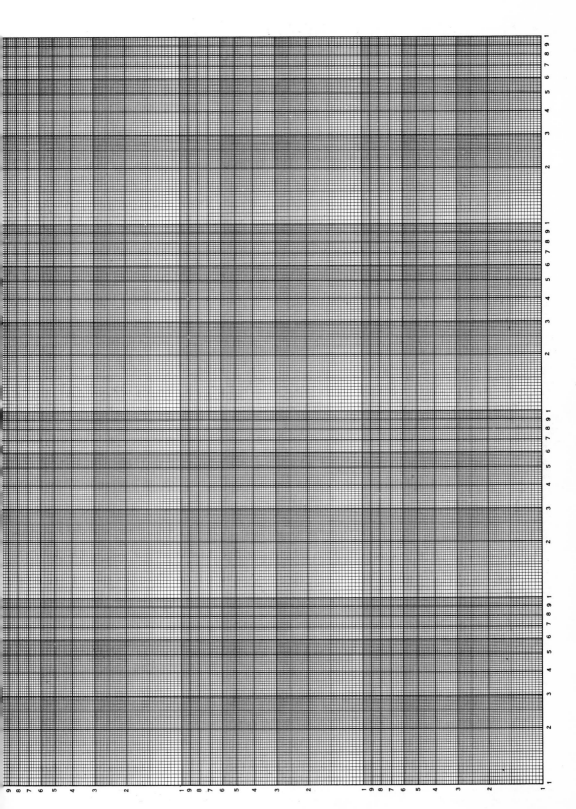

# INDEX

*Entries in italic refer to figures on those pages.*